CHARITY
IN ISLAM

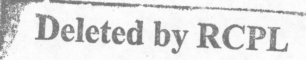

ISLAM IN PRACTICE

A Comprehensive Guide to Zakat

CHARITY
IN ISLAM

Ömer Faruk Şentürk

Translated by Erdinç Atasever

New Jersey

Published by The Light, Inc.
26 Worlds Fair Dr. Unit C
Somerset, New Jersey, 08873, USA

www.thelightpublishing.com

Library of Congress Cataloging-in-Publication Data

Senturk, Omer Faruk.
  [Soru ve cevaplarla zekat. English]
  Charity in Islam : a comprehensive guide to zakat / Omer Faruk Senturk ; trans-
lated by Erdinc Atasever.
      p. cm. -- (Islam in practice)
  "Originally published in Turkish as Soru ve cevaplarla zekat in 2006."
  Includes bibliographical references and index.
  ISBN 978-1-59784-123-8
  1. Zakat. I. Title.
  BP180.S3613 2007
  297.5'4--dc22

                                        2007001098

Printed by
Çağlayan A.Ş., Izmir - Turkey
April 2007

TABLE OF CONTENTS

INTRODUCTION

E verything hinges on faith and belief. Religious practice, social matters, and ethics are built on the foundation of faith. The prime role of Islam is helping a human being obtain a "second nature," a towering character that is formed around the conscience, through which faith imprints its embroidery on one's personal and social life. Offering each act of worship, primarily prescribed daily prayers (*salat*), fasting (*sawm*), prescribed purifying alms (*zakat*) and pilgrimage (*hajj*) with the utmost discipline is the decisive means of participating in this celestial impression. A Muslim's nearness to God and the successful maintenance of that nearness occurs as faith is bolstered by deeds and spiritual sustenance is delivered through worship. Therefore, faith is undeniably the fundamental basis for deeds, and deeds are the witness, insurance, and stronghold of faith. The safest, most acceptable, and direct way of nearness to God is performing obligatory religious duties. *Zakat* is one of these obligatory acts of worship with a prescribed time, minimum amount, prerequisites, benefactors and recipients—all perfectly explained and regulated in the Islamic jurisprudence in order to smooth the progress of its fulfillment by its adherents.

Proximity to God depends on belief and can be acquired through the performance of "righteous deeds" *(amal al-salih)*, which is fulfilling all decrees of Islam. As Islam is an undividable whole, its partial acceptance or application onto other man-made systems is not viable. Islam has its own pillars down to the tiniest detail in its integrity. Without the existence and fulfillment of the five principles Islam rests on, it is impossible to even talk about Islam or an Islamic life. As well as each of their sublime benefits upon application, the true purpose of Islam is realized only when these principles are utilized in their entirety. In this sense, *zakat* is a cornerstone of the acceptance of the Islamic faith. For *zakat*, in Islam, is simply not an arbitrary charity nor a supererogatory donation handed out according to each benefactor's wish. On the contrary, it is an obligatory (*fard*) act decreed by God Himself.

Zakat can be defined as the right possessed by the poor in the wealth of the rich, a right sternly ordained by God, the true owner of riches and property. The Qur'an and the Sunna of the Noble Messenger have both provided manifest information concerning the theoretical detail of *zakat*, both in terms of collection and allocation. In summary, *zakat's* ultimate goal is to elevate the poor in order to turn them, in time, into *zakat*-givers themselves. Considering its places of disbursement, *zakat* plays a pivotal role in helping the participants to attain innumerable spiritual, ethical, and social goals, as it is and was spent in the way of God and on those whose hearts are warmed towards Islam; slaves longing for their freedom (as *zakat* played an important role in freeing slaves in the past); those struggling in the throes of debts; and those unable to provide for themselves or their families.

As a result, the areas included in the consideration of *zakat* are far greater than those generally applied to charity in other religions. Throughout the book, issues of minor differences between Islamic Schools of Jurisdiction, which have developed in areas open to interpretive autonomy, have been highlighted. These nuances of interpretation on *zakat* stem not from the fundamentals of Islam, but rather germinate from diverse approaches to those fundamentals through naturally different cultural understandings and social environments. Special importance has been given to emphasize the unique purposes behind each verdict of jurisprudence, in addition to their enunciations, as well as presenting their corroborative proofs, primarily Qur'anic verses, hadiths, and so forth.

Ömer Faruk Şentürk
Istanbul, 2006

CHAPTER 1

What Is *Zakat*?

General Terms of the Obligatory and Voluntary Alms in Islam

A. What does ZAKAT mean?

Zakat, literally, holds numerous meanings: to profit, to purify, to increase, to be worthy, nice, mercy, truth, blessing, to extol and to exonerate are just to mention a few.[1] All of these abundant meanings can be sighted in the Qur'an and *hadith* (sayings of the Prophet Muhammad, Peace Be Upon Him).

For instance, in the following verses, *"He has indeed prospered who purifies it (the self)"*[2] and *"Prosperous indeed are those who purify themselves,"*[3] *zakat* means to purify and to exonerate, while it is also used to denote prosperity in another verse: *"A compassion from Our presence, and prosperity."*[4] Additionally, it can refer to purity itself *"...and let him see what food is purest there."*[5]

Moreover in many verses, *zakat* denotes purification, as corroborated by a hadith that uses the same word in describing the sanitization of soil.[6] Consider these references: *"...that is more virtuous for you, and purer"*, *"...for that is purer for you,"*[7] *"...and let him see what food is purest there,"*[8] *"He said 'I am only a Messenger of your Lord to announce to you the gift of a pure son,'"*[9] *"And Moses said: 'Have you slain a pure soul though he had killed nobody?'"*[10]

B. What is to be generally understood by ZAKAT in Islam?

In Islamic terminology, *zakat* is the process where a certain amount of property or money is collected from those who are sufficiently endowed and then given to needy group of people, with donors, recipients, and the proportion of required donations being clearly specified in both the Qur'an and Sunna.[11] Taking this definition into account, *zakat* (the prescribed purifying alms) is simply spending what has been bestowed by God, in the amount and places designated by Him, for the sole purpose of physical and spiritual purification.

C. WHAT IS *SADAQA* (THE VOLUNTARY ALMS)?

The term *sadaqa* carries the literal meanings of truth, acceptance and concurance.[12] Yet in the Qur'an and hadith, the word harbors meanings of greater depth as a source of extreme kindness and benevolence, along with the occasional intimation of charity toward others, or simply refraining from harmful conduct. When Yusuf's brothers implore him by saying, *"Be charitable to us,"*[13] the word they use in place of "charity" is an etymological derivative of *sadaqa*. Conversely, while designating the eight groups of *zakat* recipients[14], the word used is also an etymological derivative of *sadaqa* and alludes to *zakat*.

The profound depth of *sadaqa*'s meaning can also be verified through the fact that the word has often been used instead of *zakat* in many hadiths that elaborate the amount of *nisab* (e.i. the minimum for *zakat* becoming payable); moreover the term has been utilized to cover other meanings such as performing virtuous acts, lending a helping hand, enjoining good and prohibiting evil. The following hadith may afford us a clearer understanding of the copious meanings sheltered under one word:

> When the Messenger of God (upon him be peace and blessings) told the Companions there is *sadaqa* on every Muslim, the Companions hastily asked "O the Messenger of God! What if the Muslim couldn't afford it?" The Noble Messenger gave a counter reply "Then with his own efforts he will work, hence he will benefit himself and be charitable (*sadaqa*) to others." "What if he still couldn't afford it?" again inquired the Companions. "Then he will help those in need," explained the

Messenger. "What if he still could not possess this opportunity?" insisted the Companions. "Then he will perform good acts, protect himself from committing evil; this will also be *sadaqa* for him."[15]

The advice given by the Messenger of God to one of his Companions, Abu Dharr, is along the same lines. To receive the recommendation, Abu Dharr once asked, "O Messenger of God! What should I do, if one day, frailty and powerlessness would befall me?" The Prophet replied, "Then hold back from harming others, as indubitably, that will be a *sadaqa* for yourself."[16]

It is amply evident, the word *sadaqa*, as utilized in the Qur'an and hadith, accommodates an extensive cluster of meanings that virtually encompass a large aspect of life itself. As an Islamic concept, however, *sadaqa* is the name given to any offer, deed or presentation where the spiritual payment is expected only from God.[17] In the present day, this is the implicit understanding derived from *sadaqa*. Ultimately, if an analogous comparison were to be undertaken, the outcome would be that "Every *zakat* is *sadaqa*, although not every *sadaqa* is *zakat*."

D. What Is *INFAQ* (Spending in God's Way)?

Depending on its place of use, *infaq* may mean to become fashionable, to encourage, to intend, to decrease, to leave, to die, to cease and to spend.[18] A portion of these meanings can be found in the Qur'an and sunna. In the Qur'an, the term *"infaq"* is generally used in reference to spending.

While the term *infaq* means to run out or to end in the following verse, *"…you would have held them (treasures of mercy) back for fear of them running out,"* (Isra 17:100) it primarily indicates spending and the giving of charity in the way of God as demonstrated by the following verse: *"O you believers! Spend from what We have granted you!"* (Baqara 2:254; Munafiqun 63:10). Moreover, *infaq* embodies a variety of meanings in numerous recorded hadith. In one hadith, *infaq* denotes to encouragement and demand, whereas in another instance, it stands for the loss of blessings, "Giving fallacious vows in business eradicates its blessings."[19] It is worth mentioning that the word *infaq* is made use of in many verses that explicitly command *sadaqa* (charity) or *zakat* (prescribed purifying alms) in the way of God and this practically relates to spending in the required places when the necessity arises.[20] And though *infaq* may have coalesced with *zakat* in many aspects, it is ultimately a concept of greater depth and more substantial meaning.

E. What is USHR (the alms of agricultural produce)?

Ushr means "one-tenth;" thus every single fraction of ten is called "*ushr*."[21] "They have not been able to reach even one tenth of what We have given"[22] alludes to the shortcomings of the Meccan polytheists in their incapability of realizing their so-called power. As an Islamic concept, however, *ushr*, is considered to be a certain portion of agricultural produce, like *zakat*. Thus, in this aspect, it falls under the *zakat* heading. The calculation of *ushr* is based on the relative ease or hardship of the yield of a certain crop. Because we will scrutinize this issue further in a few chapters to come, by simply throwing a light on its cluster of benefits, for now, we will move on.

F. What is NAWAIB (supplementary alms for extraordinary circumstances)?

Though comprising several meanings such as substitution, disaster, catastrophe and misfortune, *nawaib* is the name given to the gains acquired in addition to *zakat* during extraordinary circumstances such as the dispatch of troops, maintaining national security and so on. As the designated *nisab* (the minimum wealth required to be eligible for *zakat*) is the very minimum of *zakat*, and as there is no set maximum, it is evident that when the necessity for supplementary funds arises, the tax rate may increase. This verdict can also easily be extracted from the overall message of the Qur'an, and it finds corroboration in the very practice of God's Messenger (upon whom be peace). For instance, the Noble Messenger accepted donations for the Medina Treasury in preparation for military campaigns as exemplified in the Tabuk Campaign.[23] Those wholeheartedly wanting to bequeath their entire possessions were not dissuaded during the prelude to Tabuk; however, during times of relative harmony, even the wealthiest people such as Sa'd ibn Abi Waqqas, could only have the maximum of a third of their possessions accepted by the Messenger of God (upon whom be peace).[24]

WHEN WAS *ZAKAT* DECREED OBLIGATORY?

It is a known fact that because the main area of religious focus during the Meccan period was the elucidation of the fundamental articles of faith, the jurisdictional decrees of Islam were predominantly made obligatory in the Medina Period. As an example of this, though *zakat* was touched on in some of the chapters revealed early in the Meccan Period, it was emphasized during the second year of *Hijra* (Emigration) as an act of obligatory significance.

In some of the Meccan chapters, the term *zakat* actually refers to physical and spiritual purification, in addition to its technical meaning,[25] as evidenced in particular instances when the relations between previous prophets and their peoples are described.[26] For instance, the phrase, "*they give zakat*," is a highlighted attribute of the believers in some of these passages.[27] It is further illustrated in another verse that property invested in interest based on hopes of gaining profit will in no way increase; in contrast, *zakat* that is offered just for the sake of God becomes a perpetual source of prosperity.[28] In an additional Meccan verse, the polytheists are condemned for their common characteristic of refraining from giving *zakat* and denying the hereafter.[29]

Again, another Meccan verse, after elaborating about agricultural crops and fruits, advises to "*Eat from its fruits when the seasons arrives, pay its due in harvest time and do not waste;*"[30] the effect is to establish a firm foundation for *ushr*, with an additional discernment between charity and dissipation.

Jafar ibn Abi Talib's reference to *salat* and *zakat* in his sermon to the Negus during the Abyssinian asylum of the Muslims holds extreme significance in respect to the preliminary spiritual preparation which Muslims were subjected to during the Meccan Period.[31] Although *zakat* and *salat* are predominantly mentioned together within the same phrases in the Qur'an, as far as the Meccan Period was concerned, these quite simply provided spiritual and psychological grounding for Muslims, as they awaited further enunciations and pronouncements in regards to the defining of other compulsory acts.[32]

It is strikingly clear that the Qur'an utilizes a gradual, scaffolded method in encouraging Muslims to embrace *zakat*, as it so often does when inviting humankind to follow the path it sets out for believers. The term *zakat* is granted growing significance as it is first used in numerous contexts and references in order to attract attention; then further highlighted as a common practice of the pious nations of the past; then decreed as a necessary deed for Muslims such that its evasion is viewed as a discerning attribute of unbelievers.

This type of step-wise, graded implementation of fundamental principles is a pivotal strategy of the Qur'an's distinctive and highly effective method of invitation. Through such a presentation, the Qur'an anticipates and overcomes the deep-seated and insidiously immoral habits of humankind while gently and consistently endorsing critical acts of belief like *salat*, *zakat* and *sawm* (fasting). In actual fact, this method of teaching is an expression of God's boundless mercy towards His creation, and His full knowledge of human, their material world, and their weaknesses. The lessons of the Qur'an, then, avoid any sudden coercion compelling human to assume a hoard of responsibilities that might be perceived as unattainable merely by virtue of their relative intensity. Instead, it presents these responsibilities gradually, in installments which are relatively to understand and make, educating human through a process that can only be described as an exhibition of God's perpetual and boundless benevolence.

WHAT IS THE QUR'ANIC EVIDENCE FOR THE OBLIGATION OF *ZAKAT*?

Zakat, with its specific nisab (required minimum wealth) and conditions, was decreed compulsory after the decree of fasting, in the second year of the *Hijra*, during the Medinan Period. Scores of verses pronounce, unambiguously, the obligation of *zakat*. Among these are the following examples:

> Establish *salat* and pay *zakat*...[33]
>
> They establish *salat* and pay *zakat*.[34]
>
> ...establishes *salat* and pays *zakat*.[35]
>
> If you establish *salat*, disburse *zakat* and believe in My Messengers...[36]
>
> They spend from what We have bestowed on them.[37]
>
> Take alms (*sadaqa, zakat*) of their wealth so that you may purify and sanctify them thereby, and pray for them; for you prayers are a comfort for them. God is the Ultimate Seer and Hearer.[38]
>
> Alms are only for the poor and the needy, those who collect them and those whose hearts are to be reconciled, and for the ransom of captives and debtors and for the way of God. God is Knowing, Wise.[39]

The number of verses of this kind in the Qur'an exceeds forty, and they are found in varied locations and contexts.[40]

WHAT IS THE EVIDENCE FOR THE OBLIGATION OF *ZAKAT* IN THE *SUNNA* (EXAMPLE OF THE PROPHET)?

In a lengthy and famous hadith; known as the *Jibril* (Gabriel) Hadith, found copiously in traditional hadith literature, the Messenger of God (upon whom be peace) was asked, "What is Islam?" upon which he gave the reply, "Islam is for you to worship God alone, to establish *salat*, to give the obligatory *zakat* and to fast during Ramadan,"[41] asserting again the essential requirement of almsgiving.

A delegation of Abd al-Qays, a tribe which could only visit Medina during the months of Haram (mutual armistice between the tribes of Arabia) due to assaults by the hostile Mudar, had once requested on receiving edifying advice from the Messenger of God which they could convey to their tribe and through which they could all eventually be guided to Paradise. The Messenger advised them to hold fast to four deeds, precisely to bear witness to God and the prophethood of Muhammad (upon whom be peace); to establish *salat*; to pay *zakat*; and to fast during Ramadan.[42] Similarly, the Messenger's advice to Muadh ibn Jabal before his dispatch to Yemen was as such:

> You are going to a land inhabited by the People of the Book (Christians and/or Jews). When you get there, invite them, first-ly to bear witness that there is no deity but God, and Muham-mad (upon whom be peace) is His Messenger. If they concur and accept, then inform them God has decreed five daily *salats*. If they accept this, then announce that God has made obligato-ry to take a portion of wealth possessed by the rich, to be hand-ed out to the poor. If they acknowledge this, then abstain from seizing their (the rich) finest possessions (for *zakat*) and avoid the imprecation of the oppressed; for indeed, there is no cur-tain between their imprecations and God.[43]

In the presence of the Messenger, the Companions usually steered clear of asking too many questions, as a result of their enormous and matchless respect for him. The following conversation did take place, in one of these instances, between a bedouin and the Messenger, concerning the issues of the Unity and Existence of God, daily prayers, fasting, *hajj* (pilgrimage) and *zakat*:

> The man inquired, "Your incumbent *zakat* collector insists *zakat* is necessary. What do you say?"
> "He has told the truth," responded the Messenger of God.
> "Tell me for the love of Who has sent you, did God decree this?" the man asked.

"Yes" the Messenger replied.

When the bedouin proclaimed, "I swear by He Who has truth-
fully sent you that I will perform them (the five pillars of Islam)
to their exact amount, never increasing nor decreasing them."
Then the Messenger of God declared, "He is bound for Paradise,
if he keeps his word."[44]

In another narration of the same hadith in Sahih al-Bukhari, the
following addition can be cited: "I declare my faith in entirety, to
what you have brought. I am Dimam ibn Sa'laba, an ambassador of
my tribe and brother of Sa'd ibn Bakr."[45] It is additionally renowned
that *zakat* was one of the primary clauses included in the Companions'
Pledge of Allegiance to the Messenger of God.

The Holy Prophet elucidates the fundamental nature of alms in
the succeeding hadith: "Islam is constructed on five foundations:
bearing witness that there is no deity but God and Muhammad is
the Messenger of God, establishing *salat*, giving *zakat*, *hajj* and the
fasting of Ramadan."[46]

The Messenger par-excellence explicates the Islamic credo in
the next hadith, shedding a light for his Companions and scores of
subsequent followers: "I have been commanded to strive against
humankind until they concede that there is no deity but God and
Muhammad is His Messenger, establish *salat*, and pay *zakat*. Once
they perform accordingly, they will have salvaged from me their
lives and properties, excluding the rights of Islam, and their judgment is with God."[47]

These words, delicately chosen by the Prophet in dealing with
zakat, also vehemently emphasize its significance. Though many more
proofs can be enumerated to bolster this argument, we will settle
with this much for now, as more will be expressed in upcoming
chapters.

DID *ZAKAT* EXIST IN RELIGIONS PRIOR TO ISLAM?

Past prophets have also been under obligation to take humankind
by the hand and show all the roads leading to physical and spiritu-

al ascension; thus, they too have shown the precious path of *zakat* as part of a primordial effort to diminish class differences in societies and to provide a judicious and blissful lifestyle remote from detrimental excessiveness. By virtue of providing examples of previous Prophetic applications, the Qur'an does much to put the accent on this mission. Following a brief reference in the Qur'an to the prophets Abraham, Isaac and Jacob comes the following declaration:

> And We made them leaders to guide people in accordance with Our command: We inspired in them acts of virtue, the establishment of *salat* and payment of *zakat*. They were worshippers of Us. (Anbiya 21:73)

In reference to Prophet Ishmael, the matchless significance of *salat* and *zakat* as the primordial existence of alms as an essential component of worship is underlined from early on: *"He used to enjoin his people salat and zakat, and was acceptable in the sight of his Lord"* (Maryam 19:55).

Salat and *zakat*, in actual fact, are the common denominators of all monotheistic religions, where *salat* and *zakat*, after belief in the Oneness of God, form the very core of worship. In fact, *salat* and *zakat* are, or at least were, essential characteristics of all of the great religions of the world, those guided by a long line of prophets sent by God since the dawn of humankind, despite the fact that current forms of worship in some faith communities may vary in outward appearance. In support of this, the Qur'an, adamantly states:

> They were ordered no more than to worship God with sincere devotion, to honestly establish *salat* and give *zakat*. And that is the Standard Religion." (Bayyina 98:5)

The following verse, which provides insight into how the people of Midian first received teachings of Prophet Jethro (Shuayb) teachings about obligatory *zakat*, bears testimony to its practice in preceding times:

> In sarcasm, they said, "O Jethro! Does your *salat* command you that we should abandon what our forefathers worshipped

or that we should cease doing what we like with our property? Conversely, you are pleasant and right-minded." (Hud 11:87)

The Midians' apprehension at being compelled to cease doing what they liked with their properties denotes, almost certainly, a remonstration against *zakat*. The people of the Midian, who evidently had complete appreciation for the altruistic Jethro, still could not get themselves to accept or follow Jethro's brave attempts to encourage them to perform proper *salat* or give *zakat*; branding him instead as an instigator, and a rebel. As is the usual case with similar public dissentions, the people of Midian had a ready scapegoat for giving full vent to their frustrations about the obligation of *zakat* which was, as can be seen, *salat* itself.

Even though the Qur'an does not explain, literally, whether or not each prophet carried the duty of imposing *zakat*, it is highly possible to argue for its primordial existence through the ideal notion of peace, the humane spirit of assistance and support represented and accentuated by each Messenger, beginning with the Prophet Adam, and the Qur'anic references discussed above.

In addition, despite having their initial contents altered, the Torah and the Bible still include many passages which support the proposition that *zakat* actually predates Islam. As no revelations prior to Muhammad (upon whom be peace) have survived to this day in their original forms, a fact supported even among Jewish and Christian scholars, the sole, authoritative point of reference in this argument remains the Qur'an itself. Additionally, it is worth noting that the Qur'an stresses *zakat* was enjoined as a duty on Jews and Christians, as well, not just on Muslims, as the textual references to the Qur'an which are included below will clearly demonstrate. Likewise, an analysis of the Torah and the Bible provides fascinating similarities and conformities with Islam's all-embracing concept of *zakat*.

A. CAN YOU PROVIDE INFORMATION ABOUT *ZAKAT* IN JUDAISM?

The Qur'an generally tends to speak of the Jews as somewhat "skaters on thin ice," underlining their preponderantly neglectful attitude concerning their religious responsibilities and periodically provides us a detailed account of what exactly those responsibilities were:

> And (remember) when We made a covenant with the Children of Israel, We said; "Serve none but God, show kindness to your parents and to your relatives, to the orphans and the needy; speak kindly to humankind, establish the prayer and pay the *zakat*. But with the exception of a few, you turned away and paid no heed. (Baqara 2:83)

Zakat along with *salat* is sternly recommended as a requirement for divine acquittal for their transgressions:

> God made a covenant of old with the Children of Israel, and We raised among them twelve chieftains, and God said: "I am with you. If you establish *salat* and pay the *zakat*, and believe in My Messengers and support them, and lend to God a goodly loan, surely I shall remit your sins, and surely I shall admit you into gardens beneath which rivers flow. Whosoever among you disbelieves after this has gone astray from a straight path." (Maida 5:12)

And in spite of undergoing multiple amendments, the current text of the Torah still grants us glimpses of the spirit of *zakat*, grounded on the relations between the rich and the poor:

> Jehovah has not despised or been disgusted with the plight of the oppressed one. He has not hidden His face from that person. Jehovah heard when that oppressed person cried out to Him for help. (Psalms 22:24)

> When you help the poor (needy) (lowly) (depressed) you lend to Jehovah. He will pay you back. (Proverbs 19:17)

> He who oppresses the poor reproaches his Maker. He who has mercy for the poor honors his Maker. (Proverbs 14:31)

> This is what you must do whenever there are poor Israelites in one of your cities in the land that Jehovah your God is giving you. Be generous to these poor people. Freely lend them as much as they need. Never be hardhearted and stingy with them. When

the seventh year, the year when payments on debts are canceled, is near, you might be stingy toward poor Israelites and give them nothing. Be careful not to think these worthless thoughts. The poor will complain to Jehovah about you, and you will be condemned for your sin. Give the poor what they need, because then Jehovah will make you successful in everything you do. (Deutoronomy 15:7-12)

He who gives to the poor will not lack. But he who hides his eyes will have many curses. (Proverbs 28:27)

And if you give yourself to the hungry and satisfy the desire of the afflicted, then your light will rise in darkness and your gloom will be like midday. (Isaiah 58:10)

He who gets ahead by oppressing the poor and giving to the rich will certainly suffer loss. (Proverbs 22:16)

It is certainly easy, by and large, to draw a connection between the above verses and many Qur'anic passages, not to mention the conspicuously striking similarities between some. It is these considerable parallels that lead us to the conclusion that the ideas and instructions all stem from the same source, God, and that the essential issues concerning humankind have, quite surprisingly, undergone very little change despite human's apparent weakness as a transmitter over time.

One further point deserves mention. The above quotations gathered from the Torah, as well as the upcoming Biblical passages, are from current versions of the texts which have, as is widely accepted and was noted above, been partially or predominantly altered, though the exact extent and manner in which such changes have been brought to these ancient scriptures is a matter for debate. A tentative and prudent approach to the current versions is thus the correct attitude, as recommended wisely by the Prophet Muhammad (upon whom be peace) himself:

When the People of the Book utter a narration, do not agree nor disagree with them, but say, "We only believe in God and His

Messengers." This way, concurrence is avoided if they speak lies, and denial is avoided provided that they speak the truth.[48]

B. Is there information about *ZAKAT* in Christianity?

The situation in Christianity is no different, for the Prophet Jesus, while still in the cradle, utters the duties obliged onto him by God in the following manner:

> (Whereupon) he (the baby) spoke out: "I am indeed a servant of God. He has given me the Scripture and has appointed me a prophet. And He has made me blessed whereever I may be and has commanded me to pray and to give alms to the poor as long as I live. And (He) has made me dutiful to my mother and has not made me oppressive, wicked. So peace be upon me the day I was born and the day that I die and the day that I shall be raised up to life (again)." (Maryam 19:30-33)

Considering the fact that the Bible predominantly focuses on ethical issues, a jurisprudential adherence to the Torah, so to speak, was a social necessity. Nonetheless, there are copious Biblical verses which themselves allude to *zakat* and *sadaqa*. The following passages may throw light on this discussion; of course, the possible alterations to these passages must be kept in mind:

> Be careful! Do not display your righteousness (good works) before men to be noticed by them. If you do, you will have no reward with your heavenly Father. Do not loudly announce it when you give to the poor. The hypocrites do this in the houses of worship and on the streets. They do this to be praised by men. Believe me, they have already been paid in full. When you give charity, do not let your left hand know what your right hand is doing. (Matthew 6:1-3)

> He looked at him and was afraid. "What is it, Lord?" he replied. The angel said: "God hears your prayers and sees your gifts of mercy. (Acts 10:4)

> He said: Cornelius, your prayer is heard and your gifts of mercy are noticed in the sight of God. (Acts 10:31)

Jesus then replied: "If you wish to be complete, go sell your possessions and give the money to the poor. You will have wealth in heaven. Then follow me!" But hearing these words, the young man went away grieving, for he was very wealthy. Jesus said to his disciples: "Truly I tell you, it is hard for a man with much money to go into the kingdom of heaven. Again I say, it is easier for a camel to go through a needle's eye, than for a man with much money to go into the kingdom of God." (Matthew 19:21-24)

Sell your possessions and give to charity. Make yourselves purses that do not get old, a treasure in heaven where moth and rest cannot corrupt and thieves cannot steal. (Luke 12:33)

And if I give all my possessions to feed the poor, and surrender my body to be burned, but do not have love, I gain nothing. (Corinthians 13:3)

Woe to you, scribes and Pharisees, hypocrites! You tithe mint and dill and cumin, and have left undone the weightier matters of the law: justice, mercy and faith. You should do both and leave nothing undone. (Matthew 23:23)

It is thus quite possible to, again, draw connections between the Qur'an and Hadith, on the one hand, and many Biblical passages. The level of conspicuous similarities between the above texts accentuates their unity of origin. Adopting this approach in scrutinizing the Torah and the Bible will, undeniably, offer us much more evidence culminating in the very same conclusion.

WHAT IS THE GENERAL VALUE GIVEN TO ZAKAT IN ISLAM?

The Qur'an advises us to perform *salat*, the *zakat* of our bodies, with utmost gracefulness, elegance and precision, while we are instructed to offer *zakat* from that which God has benevolently bestowed on us in order to achieve social peace and bliss. To spend what God has given us, as commanded by Him, constitutes a full acceptance of the ethic of God. Indubitably, God will spare those who have fully embraced Him, and ultimately will reward them accordingly.

Zakat is one of the five pillars upon which Islam is built. Without the presence of these pillars, it is impossible to even describe Islam. The Noble Messenger, as narrated, had forbidden his commanders to launch military campaigns in territories where the Adhan (the call for prayer) is heard, a practice confirming their religious status as believers. The subsequent policy of the first caliph Abu Bakr, in taking arms against whoever denied *zakat*, regardless of their submissiveness of other pillars like *salat* and *sawm* (fasting), is entirely in concordance with the spirit of Islam and further emphasizes the enormous magnitude and importance of *zakat*.

In the Qur'an, *zakat* is incessantly mentioned alongside with *salat*, as an explicit reference to the miraculous spiritual ascension achieved by humankind through prayer, which is further completed with a marvelous blessing that springs forth from almsgiving. In this way, material is granted eternity in a world of mortality, an aspect highlighted in the Qur'an:

> Establish *salat* and pay *zakat*. Whatever good you send beforehand for yourselves you will find it with God. (Baqara 2:110)

How was the economic life in the time of the Prophet (upon whom be peace)?

From the start of Muhammad's (upon whom be peace) prophethood, almost to the very end of his life—and especially in the Meccan Era—the Muslims suffered great economic distress. The Messenger of God had forsaken all his belongings, along with the wealth of his generous and compassionate wife, Khadija, in calling people to God. The first Muslims were, in fact, mostly the poor. As for the wealthy Muslims, they were constantly more than ready to sacrifice all they had for the success of the Islamic cause; and so they did. It could be argued, in fact, that economic encumbrances, by and large, endured until the victory at Hunayn.

In a further elaboration, an exceptionally simple and modest lifestyle prevailed during the time of the Prophet (upon whom be peace) although the dynamic monetary activity resulting from the treasury's precise inflow and outflow balance was paramount.

In tandem with being enthusiastically active in the endeavor to get people to elevate themselves through the blissful path of *iman,* untainted faith in God, the Noble Messenger also intimately dealt with problems surrounding the society's economic life. He worked tirelessly to cleanse it from the insidious residues of pre-Islamic life. As a culmination of this precious struggle, the fresh Muslim society embarked on an elevating journey that was soon to reach its zenith.

Virtue, a fundamental principle of model societies, is an ideal that inevitably must be sought. In this sense, the era of the Prophet (upon whom be peace) provides us with a splendid example of the revival and the consequential pervasiveness of virtue in all aspects of life, especially in the struggle to eliminate the unjust earning of money and other corrupt financial transactions, in order to achieve an uncompromising adherence to the Qur'an: *"...and each can have nothing save what he strives for, and that his effort will be seen"* (Najm 53:39-40).

In conformance with the Qur'an, the Noble Prophet himself illustrated the ideal method of earning money; "A person has never gained better sustenance than what he has gained through his own sweat. Indeed, the Prophet David earned his sustenance himself."[49] To cultivate the seeds of magnanimity in the souls of the Companions, the Messenger of God added: "It is much more beneficial for one to carry timber from mountains, to earn a living, than to beg off others, as those who are beseeched either give or refuse."[50] These words were of tremendous importance for a society whose members aligned their conducts according to divine regulations, and experienced enormous bliss and contentment from doing so. Most certainly, advice such as this had swift practical implications. Once, for instance, a Companion on horseback dropped his stick; yet he refrained from asking assistance from those standing next to him, opting instead to descend from his horse and gather the stick himself. Even asking for assistance, then, was interpreted as a form of begging.

Moreover, usury, a devastating burden fracturing the very back-bone of society, was being abolished, thus granting each person a total economic emancipation. In a previously unseen race for virtue, many exemplary actions stood out, from people working in hard labor just to give their earnings to charity, to people voluntarily lending interest-free money to others in hope of benefiting from the blessings of such a praiseworthy act.[51] The hadith "Muslims, in love and compassion for one another, are like a single body. If one limb is in agony, the whole body joins that limb in insurmountable pain and sleeplessness,"[52] provided a practical guide for heroes sacrificing their comfort and luxury for the well-being of the whole community.

The economic purification did not stop there. An incredible balance was achieved in expenses and consumption, and extravagance, along with its destructive blemishes, became remote concepts. On the other hand, abandoning even the necessary requirements for spending in the cause of Islam became habitual. These acts of virtue were all a dazzling culmination of the Companions' exceptionally thorough comprehension of Islam, imparted to them by the Messenger of God. Along these lines, a Muslim's life must be in absolute conformity with divine guidelines, keeping a sufficient distance from the type of dissipative spending that incurs the anger of God and the envy of others. A spending with no worthy result, one that neither acts as an instigator for a potentially beneficial movement nor serves as a catalyst to spark the dead wood of society, has no place in a Muslim's life. The era of the Noble Prophet can thus be summarized as an epitome of this resuscitative spirit.

During this period, hatred and vengeance among Muslims were averted as each person played a vital role in socially constructive activities. Because Islam was vividly being enforced in all aspects of life, class struggles became a thing of the past and there was a general diminution of communal vices until, ultimately, the wealthy experienced the utmost difficulty in even trying to locate poor individuals upon which they could disburse their accumulated *sadaqa* and *zakat*—quite simply, after a while, poverty virtually ceased to exist.

This issue, in fact, figured prominently in the government's agenda, as they had the increasingly difficult task of locating the poor lest the wealthy be deprived of the virtues of almsgiving.

The Meccan Era was, in a sense, filled with furtiveness. In the beginning, the call for Islam had not been undertaken overtly, thus there was no clear-cut information available regarding the financial status of the newly-forming "Golden Generation," the Companions, as well as no system yet in place for systematically collecting or disbursing wealth. The Messenger of God (upon whom be peace) had hastened the disbursement of capital in required places during this period as the early Muslim community were incessantly suffering financial hardships that continued through the early years of the Medinan Period before times of abundant prosperity arrived in later years. The treasury became filled with *zakat*, *sadaqa*, and *ushr* in addition to the riches gathered from rapid conquests. Under these changing circumstances, the Noble Prophet (upon whom be peace), on behalf of the Muslim treasury, relentlessly maintained a perfect balance in financial activities, utilizing resources in the required places in a most delicate and efficient manner. Even when observing the horde of items granted to the *muallafa al-qulub* (those whose hearts are being reconciled with Islam) in the aftermath of the victory at the battle of Hunayn, this meticulous balance, remote from dissipation, can evidently be noted.[53]

It is also worthy to note that gold and silver, with their independent values, were then the most prevalent coins in circulation. *Dinar* and *dirham* were subordinate currencies used especially in trade and commerce, not to mention the additional widespread use of barter.

The spiritual resurrection in Islam had been reflected in the bazaars and markets and then onto the entire economy, imparting the gist of the Islamic spirit that attests to the potentiality of all things and thus fiercely rejects dead investments, usury and selfish accumulations of piles of gold and silver. The female Companions, unhesitant in donating all their precious jewelry in time of excessive hardship, provide an excellent example of this spirit and reality.[54]

HOW WAS *ZAKAT* ORGANIZED IN THE TIME OF THE PROPHET (UPON WHOM BE PEACE)?

The Qur'an's emphasis on *zakat* collectors as being among the recipients of alms implicitly alludes to the prime role of governments in *zakat* collection.[55] Muadh ibn Jabal's official role in collecting *zakat* is a fact attested to by authentic sources. The general practice of the Companions was to hand the *zakat* over to the treasury via collectors, a practice that endured after the death of the Noble Prophet (upon whom be peace), during the periods of Caliphs Abu Bakr and Umar.[56] The following are some of the Companions who were given the duty of collecting *zakat* by the Messenger of God: Muadh ibn Jabal,[57] Umar,[58] Ubayy ibn Qa'b,[59] Zayd ibn Haritha,[60] Ibn al-Lutaybiya,[61] Mahmiya b. Jaz,[62] Abu Rafi,[63] Qays ibn Sa'd ibn Ubada,[64] Muhammad ibn Maslama,[65] and Ubada ibn Thamit,[66] may God be pleased with them all.

The likes of Anas ibn Malik,[67] Abdullah ibn Sa'd,[68] and Imran ibn Husayn[69] also figure prominently as *zakat* collectors during the caliphates of Abu Bakr and Umar.

HOW WAS ZAKAT TAKEN CARE OF IN THE ERA OF THE RIGHTLY GUIDED CALIPHS?

The stern and unrelenting approach of Caliph Abu Bakr, in relation to *zakat*, emphasizes its compulsory nature as well as manifesting its social vitality. Maintaining an uncompromising stance against those evading the obligation under various pretexts, he even proclaimed war, if necessary, against those rejecting the scantiest amount of the minimum collected at the time of the Noble Prophet (upon whom be peace). Abu Hurayra, a close companion of the Messenger, narrates the subsequent conversation:

> Abu Bakr, having assumed leadership after the death of the Beloved Prophet, vowed to wage war on those in defiance of *zakat*. Umar, a pivotal vanguard of the Companions, objected by reminding, "O Abu Bakr! How can you wage war when the Noble Prophet informed us he had been ordered with persever-

ance until people proclaimed, 'There is no God but God,' after which their lives and properties came under the protection of Islam and their reckonings with God." Abu Bakr relentlessly insisted, "I swear by God that I will surely fight those who discern between *salat* and *zakat*, as *zakat* is the right of property. Even if they were to hold back a goat (as *zakat* upon such animals as sheep or goats), that they consentingly gave at the time of the Prophet, I will fight to forbid them of such an act." Umar, then declared in admiration, "By God, this is nothing but a divine inspiration in the heart of Abu Bakr. I have understood that these are the correct steps to take."[70]

Abu Bakr's admirable resolution and depth in regards to these issues successfully dispersed insidious notions that separated *salat* and *zakat* and culminated in the essential and continued functioning of this vital pillar of Islam. Companions such as Umar[71] and Abu Ubayda[72] took active part, during the period of Abu Bakr, in *zakat* collection.

The treasury, a relative nucleus in the time of the Prophet (upon whom be peace), was further organized and systemized as a result of escalations in general income and the size of the populace during the caliphate of Umar.

Abdullah ibn Arqam, placed in charge of the treasury by Umar, held this position through the early years of the next caliph, Uthman[73], and then was succeeded by Zayd ibn Thabit.[74] Abu Rafi is referred to as the minister of treasury during the period of the fourth pious caliph, Ali.[75]

The era of Umar ibn Abdulaziz, who was spiritually though not chronologically regarded as the fifth pious caliph, provided a period where *zakat* recipients ceased to exist, the ultimate result of the brilliant and thorough application of this institution. This was an exemplary time in history, in fact, miraculously heralded by the Prophet (upon whom be peace) decades ago: "Offer alms; as there will soon come a time when a person, carrying his *zakat* in his hand, will roam around in futility, in pursuit of a recipient as the intended recipient will refuse and say 'If you offered this yesterday, I would have accepted, but now I'm in no need of it.'"[76] "A time will come when a man carrying his *sadaqa* of gold, will roam around to find someone to give it to but in vain."[77]

The Noble Messenger had further elaborated this issue by stating that the day of Day of Judgment will not commence until such a time of prosperity is realized.[78] The era of Umar ibn Abdulaziz epitomizes this realization, announced beforehand by the Beloved Prophet himself. *Zakat* had, indeed, reached its functional goal, elevating the poor to a stable middle-class, liberating them in time from financial dependence. As a consequence, people in need of *zakat* were no longer to be found and therefore, as a final option, the government had to accept *zakat* on behalf of the needy during this time of unmatched prosperity.

TOTALITY IN WORSHIP

Islam, as a system, is an undividable whole, and it is founded on five principles of which an absence of any renders Islam obsolete. Only in the greater part of the Meccan Period, which was rather a time of transition, were the followers exempt from performing certain deeds; however, one must recall the pervasive characteristic of this period where believers were granted time for the pillars of faith to profoundly sink in their hearts. In other words, there was a psychological training in preparation for the major tasks to come. Nevertheless, after a firmly ensconced belief in God was successfully achieved, true adherents—whose numbers grew steadily at an astounding rate—considered not even a trivial compromise with regards to upholding and observing all of these pillars.

These five cornerstones of Islam are enunciated by the Prophet (upon whom be peace) in the following manner:

> Islam is constructed on five foundations: "Bearing witness that there is no deity but God and Muhammad is the Messenger of God, establishing *salat*, giving *zakat*, hajj and the fasting of Ramadan.[79]

In another Hadith, the Messenger of God unequivocally declares:

I have been commanded to strive against humankind until they concede that there is no deity but God and Muhammad is His Messenger, establish *salat*, pay *zakat*. Once they perform accordingly, they will have salvaged, from me, their lives and properties, excluding the rights of Islam, and their judgment is with God.[80]

A sharp contrast emerges when the precepts of this hadith are compared with the events that took place during the era of Abu Bakr—hence the source of inspiration for Abu Bakr's uncompromising attitude against those who denied *zakat* as their obligation even so soon after the death of the Prophet (upon whom be peace).

All of these five pillars are inextricably intertwined with one another and the full, intended benefits of Islam are only received upon the application, if strength permits, of all of them. Once they are known and understood, the denial of one or more of these essential principles divulges, in fact, a problem in faith.

CHAPTER 2

What Are the Benefits of *Zakat*?

Z *akat* is multi-faceted practice. Performing their obligations on one hand, individuals safeguard themselves from many spiritual and physical troubles and suffering on the other. In fact, from the perspective of both the benefactor and the recipient, the benefits on an individual through *zakat* can generally be summed up with the following categorizations:

WHAT BENEFITS ARE THERE FOR THE BENEFACTOR?

As the Arabic word *mal*, meaning property, is an etymological derivative of *mayl*, meaning inclination, it can be argued that a person who offers *zakat*, by virtue of sacrificing a portion of his/her owned wealth, has turned away from the natural love of riches preferring to incline, so to speak, towards God. The eternal reward for such a meaningful sacrifice will, no doubt, only be truly conceived in the afterlife.

A. *ZAKAT* BRINGS ONE CLOSER TO GOD

The minimum amount of *zakat* and its specific places of disbursement have unequivocally been delineated in the Qur'an. The person, through *zakat*, enters a perennially blissful path, attaining proximity to God, an aspect eloquently illustrated in the following *Hadith Qudsi* (the wording is the Prophet's, but the meaning belongs to God):

> My servant cannot draw near Me with a more pleasant act than performing obligatory deeds. With supererogatory deeds, he will come so close to Me that I will become fond of him. And once I become fond of him, I will be his ears that hear, eyes that

see, hands that seize and feet that walk. If he beseeches Me, I will grant his wish. If he seeks refuge in Me, I will protect him.[1]

Zakat, a deed of distinguished virtue, elevates a person spiritually to a position of closer proximity to God, through the development of admirable traits, mainly generosity and benevolence. As understood from several hadiths of the Noble Prophet (upon whom be peace), generosity carries a person away from vices, thus taking him closer to God. "The generous is close to God, to paradise, and to society and distant from hell. The miser is remote from God and from society and close to hell. A generous ignorant is closer to God than an educated miser."[2]

Generosity is essentially a reverberation of *Jawad*, one of the Beautiful Names of God, which means "The Ultimate Generous." The degree of one's success in imitating these Divine Names determines the degree of benefit attained on his behalf. It is precisely mentioned in one hadith, "God is *Jawad* and loves generosity; and as much as He is fond of morality, He equally despises immorality."[3]

B. *Zakat* PREVENTS MISERLINESS

The love of property has intrinsically been a part of human inclination for many concealed purposes. Overindulgence in this fondness, however, will indubitably result in a shameful dissipation. This innate inclination possessed by human, in which overexploitation leads to miserliness, is highlighted in the Qur'an: *"...Human souls are prone to selfish avarice"* (Nisa 4:128).

In history, miserliness has been the sole culprit in the destruction of many civilizations, as reiterated by the Messenger of God:

> Beware of miserliness, as those before you were ruined because of it. Their rulers enjoined miserliness, the public acted in accordance; their rulers ordered them to sever kindred ties, the public hastened to severe; their rules commanded transgression which they immediately saw to."[4]

One of the etymological derivatives of *zakat* is *tazkiya*, signifying purification. It purifies the poor of envy and hatred and conversely, purges the sinister disease of miserliness from the spirit of the rich. The acknowledgement of the rights of others in property, a notion that *zakat* inherently conveys, unfetters the benefactor from material obsession. Stinginess, a detrimental disorder, suffers defeat as the giver embraces the perception that what is given by God is simply to be spent in the manner, or location, desired by Him. The departure of miserliness from a person results in the arrival of an even greater fondness of God:

> So keep your duty to God as best you can, and listen, and obey,
> and spend: that is better for your souls. And those who are saved
> from their own greed will surely prosper. (Taghabun 64:16)

Thoughtlessly withholding what is granted by God, then, is virtually treading on dangerous territory, as exhibited via the following Qur'anic admonition:

> And let not those who hoard up that which God has bestowed
> upon them of His bounty think that is better for them. It is
> worse for them. That which they hoard will be their collar on the
> Day of Resurrection. God's is the inheritance of the heaven and
> the earth, and God is aware of what you do. (Al Imran 3:180)

C. *ZAKAT* IS A MEANS FOR MERCY

Zakat is a major instrument in attracting the mercy of God, as those who achieve His eternal compassion are, justifiably, those who observe divine commands. Nurturing compassion for others through taking care of their needs is, no doubt, a means to attaining that limitless treasure—Celestial Mercy. The Noble Prophet (upon whom be peace) has highlighted this fact: "God treats with compassion those who treat each other with compassion. For that reason, have mercy on the earthly, so the Heavenly has mercy on you."[5] The Qur'an reinstates the mercy attracting aspect of *zakat*:

My mercy embraces all things; therefore I shall ordain it for those who ward off (evil) and pay the *zakat*, and those who believe in Our signs (revelations)." (A'raf 7:156)

Establish the prayer and pay the *zakat* and obey the Messenger, that perhaps you may find mercy. (Nur 24:56)

The Noble Messenger has further illustrated how charitable acts are virtually a magnet for the mercy of God: "Whoever has gathered, within himself, these four attributes will be immersed in God's mercy and granted Paradise: Protecting the poor, assisting the weak, kindness towards the slave and charitable towards the parents."[6] It should be stressed that all these praiseworthy acts entail, more or less, a degree of finance.

Zakat also acts as a shield, vigorously protecting the giver against numerous pitfalls of the soul; in such a way, it is another manifestation of Divine Compassion. However, if *zakat* ceases to be observed, the benefits may well be withdrawn, as pointed out by the Prophet: "The Celestial gates of compassion will shut on those who disregard *zakat*, depriving them of rain. Surely, if it weren't for the roaming beasts, they would receive none of it (rain)."[7]

The truth is that *zakat* is a strong means, now and the Hereafter, of procuring the boundless compassion of God. Wherever *zakat* is observed, animals also obtain a share in this divine feast of mercy; and in places where the observance of *zakat* has fallen, animals remain the only reason for the provision of rain, as the inhabitants have ignorantly slammed shut the gates of mercy by their disregard of the obligation of *zakat*.

D. *ZAKAT* IS PURITY

Zakat is a process which yields a thorough purification. The provider, as well as the recipient, rid themselves of potential "dirt." It forestalls a potential insurgency by the poor by eliminating any possible cause for social dissent and thus provides greater security for wealth through offering a small levy. In a hadith, *zakat* and *sadaqa* are labeled as "the dirt of humans (i.e. their wealth),"[8] as wealth is only purified by giving up of a portion of the wealth one may possess so that they purify what they retain of their wealth after the extraction of *zakat*. In a sense, *zakat* is what cleanses wealth and what grants its provider a complete liberation from miserliness and all its insidious upshots. *Zakat* also demolishes the greed and avarice which is fed by the spurious illusion of worldly immortality. As for the recipients, *zakat* eradicates the potential hate and envy they may foster towards the wealthy as they succumb to the generosity of the hands offering them alms. A possible rebellion against God, due to unheeded destitution, is thus sturdily forestalled by *zakat*—a surfacing of its psychological cleansing.

Purity, the root meaning of the term *zakat*, implies a broad purification—an aim directly pointed to in the Qur'an: *"Take alms of their wealth to purify and to sanctify them thereby..."* (Tawba 9:103). The process of purification and sanctification here may have been ascribed to the Noble Prophet himself; if so, then he becomes the instrument that purifies and sanctifies; or, it may be ascribed to alms, in which case there is no mediator.

In declaring, "God has decreed *zakat* compulsory to purify our accumulated wealth,"[9] the Messenger of God has emphasized the same aspect. At the same time, the Messenger of God, his family and progeny were forbidden to receive *zakat* or *sadaqa*, as elaborated by the Prophet himself: "These alms are nothing but the dirt of humans (i.e. their properties and wealth); they are neither permissible to Muhammad nor his progeny."[10]

E. *ZAKAT* GRANTS PROSPERITY

Although property of which *zakat* is given may seem to decrease, in actual fact, it ceaselessly increases through the blessing of God. As the True and Ultimate Possessor of the seen and unseen treasures, the Almighty God ensures that the ways of wealth increase for those who provide *zakat*, a divine assistance which is constantly evidenced in the lives of a believer.

Hearts are in the absolute control of God. When He wills and desires, He can, with utmost ease, channel the hearts to do trade and transact with those who pay *zakat*, thus causing a spell-binding revival in their capital. This is nothing but the priceless prosperity attached to *zakat*. This is not a mere benefit accrued from business experience; rather it is a guarantee from God and a soothing echo of His Messenger (upon whom be peace). In the Qur'an, the Almighty declares:

> That which you give in usury in order that it may increase on people's property has no increase with God; but that which you give in charity, seeking God's countenance, has a manifold increase." (Rum 30:39)

In effect, this reproaches those who invest unethically in interest with the aim of procuring profit in direct opposition to the stern decree of God, Who praises the payers of *zakat*, and guarantees them an everlasting reward in the Eternal Abode. In another verse, it is stated: *"God blights usury and makes almsgiving fruitful; He does not love the impious and guilty"* (Baqara 2:276). The Qur'an elaborates the issue further: *"Say: "Indeed my Lord enlarges the provision for whom He wills of His bondsmen, and narrows it for him. And whatsoever you spend for good He replaces it. And He is the Best of Providers"* (Saba 34:39).

Both Satan and one's own self (*nafs*) play a major role in pushing a person away from performing this obligation, fallaciously instilling the belief that *zakat* may cause a decrease in wealth, resulting in poverty. God, the Benevolent, accords us the following advice against this kind of deception: *"Satan frightens you with poverty and commands you towards immorality. But God promises you His forgiveness and His bounty"* (Baqara 2:268).

The Messenger of God has said, "*Sadaqa* never causes loss in your wealth,"[11] in conformance, as always, with the Qur'an. Two things, at least, must be understood from all this: firstly, the prosperity of God ultimately replenishes the trivial loss of capital; and secondly, *zakat* results in abundant rewards for even a small deed.

In essence, then, *zakat* is a process of insuring the continuance of wealth rather than its loss, as highlighted by the Prophet: "Protect your wealth through zakat, cure your ill with sadaqa and be ready, against misfortunes, with *dua* (prayer)."[12] "Offer charity, so you may also be granted charity"[13] and "God, the Compassionate takes the pure *sadaqa* offered, and surely He only accepts what is pure, and bestows on it such a prosperity that even it be a date, it grows larger than Mount Uhud."[14] This quote explicitly denotes the marvelous blessing attracted through sincere *zakat*. In fact, the angels offer their daily prayers for the increase of the property out of which *zakat* has been offered as, again, informed by the Prophet: "Two angels descend each day; one of them praying 'O God! Bestow prosperity on the wealth of those who are charitable,' and the other imploring, 'O God! Destroy the wealth of the miser.'"[15]

F. *ZAKAT* ETERNALIZES WEALTH

The Earth is mortal and so are its inhabitants. Just as nothing on Earth is immortal, the Earth itself is destined for nothingness, firmly locked in the hands of mortality. Even more certain is the fact that wealth, along with its accumulators, are sooner or later, bound to say farewell. Thus the Earth is merely like an inn, found on a highway that takes the traveler to the pre-planned abode. However great a person's wealth may be, the time allocated for benefiting from it is extremely small. Human's lust for eternity and riches are feelings, cultivated to encourage and prepare them for their ultimate abode, the afterlife; this innate lust is so powerful that even all the world's riches would be inadequate in satiating it.

By no means does this pose a dead end for human. Investing their temporal possessions in the afterlife gives them a precious opportunity to channel this lust towards a place that is bound to offer profits of unthinkable magnitude. There are two essentials in this investment of possession: first, life and wealth are utilized in the way of God; and second, they are sacrificed when and if required. This remains the only method to endow the soul with the riches of eternity and to procure magnificent rewards in the process. It is quite appropriate, at this point, to recall the Qur'anic words in the relation, *"Yet if they repent and establish the salat and pay the zakat, then they shall become your brothers in religion. Thus We explain the revelations in detail for those who know"* (Tawba 9:11).

During the Aqaba Pledge where the Medinan Muslims swore allegiance to the Prophet (upon whom be peace), when the Companions had inquired what was in store for them upon acceptance, the Noble Prophet responded, "Paradise!"[16] *Sadaqa* and *zakat*, then, swiftly commences in this world a process of eternalizing property in preparation for the hereafter, as stressed by the Messenger (upon whom be peace): "My wealth, my wealth" cries the Children of Adam but alas O Children of Adam! Have you really any wealth except for what you have consumed, what you have worn and what you have donated as *sadaqa*."[17] In a sense, the wealth that is spent on Earth through *sadaqa* and *zakat* evolve into prosperous assets for the afterlife.

G. *ZAKAT* PREVENTS HOARDING WEALTH

Stockpiling, through stowing accumulated wealth, is virtually an economic menace to the greater part of society; thus, Islam's negative view of it is no surprise. The unethical process of stocking away certain goods by certain people causes an abnormal plummeting in prices; hence, the avarice of the minority deprives the majority. This is blatantly unjust and its insidious effects on society are amply evident, and ominous. Islam, through *zakat* and other cures, relentlessly seeks to purge from society even the minor existence of such a notion. *"...those who hoard up gold and silver and do not spend it in the way of God, give them the glad tidings of a painful punishment"* (Tawba 9:34). Stockpiling, namely the process in which certain cunning steps are taken in an insatiable quest to hoard greater wealth, indoctrinates its culprit with spurious illusions of profit and thus he excitedly anticipates the realization of it. The Qur'anic reproach, from this perspective, is quite ironic, heralding stashers a rather different result than what they expect: *"...give the glad tidings unto them of a painful punishment."* The delicate use of words in the Qur'an, as perhaps epitomized in this instance, accentuates its matchless rhetorical prowess.

The Messenger of God has, in fact, described how gold and silver on which *zakat* was not paid will be instruments of torment for its hoarder in the afterlife, used to brand the owners after it is heated in fire. Again, livestock such as camel, cattle, sheep, horse and etc. that have been deliberately excluded in the calculation of *zakat*, in the hereafter, will become enlarged, agonizing their owners through fierce sessions of biting, chewing and gnawing.[18] This could only be regarded as a just outcome, as the perpetrators will reap what they have sowed, thereby paying the ultimate price for their socially inconsiderate postures.

In another hadith, the Prophet illustrates the following image: "If a person financially eligible for *zakat* refuses, then his wealth, in the hereafter, will embody the appearance of snake, bold from excessive poison. The man will flee, only to find that each time the snake is relentlessly breathing down his neck; and it will be exclaimed to him, 'This is your wealth which you were so stingy over!' Finally, realizing there is no chance of escaping, the man will helplessly insert his hand into the snake's mouth, whereby the snake will commence torturing him by gnawing his hand like a camel chewing crop."[19]

The same hadith, as cited in al-Bukhari,[20] includes the following addition:

> The snake will bite on the person's Adam's apple and repetitiously state, "I am your wealth, I am your treasure," and then recite the subsequent verse:

> And let not those who hoard up that which God has bestowed upon them of His bounty think that it is better for them. It is worse for them. That which they hoard will be their collar on the Day of Resurrection. The inheritance of the heavens and the earth is God's, and He is aware of what you do. (Al Imran 3:180)

All this must not be conceived as discouragement or dissuasion from attaining wealth; on the contrary, it is just a reminder to a Muslim of the pivotal responsibilities ascribed to moneymaking—responsibilities that must strike firm root in a Muslim's heart. Besides, *zakat* purifies the wealth of property, however great it may be, as underlined by the Noble Prophet:

> Even if it is buried, wealth on which *zakat* is offered is not a treasure; wealth on which *zakat* is not paid for is treasure, even if it is exposed.[21]

> After reaching the minimum amount, wealth out of which *zakat* is offered is no treasure.[22]

> The payer of *zakat* has paid his debt. To give more is of more virtue.[23]

> When you offer *zakat*, the potential harm from your wealth is dispelled.[24]

> Paying *zakat* is paying your due[25]

Together with saving wealth from becoming stowed treasure which is condemned by God, *zakat* also dispels possible ill feelings of the public towards the wealthy.

H. *ZAKAT* HINDERS INSATIABLE DESIRES

Human has been created as a candidate for eternal pleasure, a fact attested to by his eternal desires. When human lacks the transcendental dimension of eternity, all his engrained desires become augmented here on Earth alone, causing an exaggerated terrestrial bond. The Prophet of God expands this aspect in the following words:

> If the Children of Adam possessed a valley of gold, they would desire a second (valley of gold). Only soil will quench their greed (i.e their greed will only cease when they are dead and subsequently buried).[26]

> As the Children of Adam grows, two characteristics concomitantly grow with them: the love of riches and endless desires.[27]

The existence of love, in human, for the world and attachment to it as well as his endless desires are for the cultivation of the world. If a delicate balance is not established, however, the outcome is either excessive or recessive, vis-à-vis, an insatiable love for the world or a complete abandoning of it. In actual fact, Islam condones neither of these perceptions, promulgating the establishment of that perfect balance between the two. Undoubtedly, *zakat* is a major catalyst in procuring ideal moderation in terms of keeping wealth versus sharing it—and between the rich and the poor. Thus, it is an ultimate reminder of the hereafter for human, in whom the seeds of worldly love and never-ending desires perennially exist, though through *zakat*, we grow in accordance with the divine will, incessantly facing the eternal abode with the unshakeable belief in the receipt of an enormous reward for even the most trivial deeds. This can be deemed, in a sense, to allow transcending the shallow walls erected by worldliness, and submitting to the boundless domain of spirituality. *Zakat* reiterates the utter impossibility of an eternal life on earth, ameliorating the feelings of separation by virtue of preparing the person for an inescapable resurrection and thus encouraging us towards the afterlife. And this is, by no means, a small gain for human. For many concealed purposes, the Almighty has rendered earth and its contents alluring, but at the same time, desires humankind to comprehend the test and take heed accordingly:

> Made beautiful for humankind is the love of desires, for women and offspring, of hoarded treasures of gold and silver, of branded horses, cattle and plantations. These are the comforts of this life; yet with God is the best of all goals. (Al Imran 3:14)

The above-mentioned verse delineates the aspects of human's innate inclination but in addition, displays the correct approach to be adopted. The potentially destructive intrinsic feelings of worldly love and endless desires are powerfully hindered by the acceptance of others' rights in property and the acknowledgement of God, the Ultimate Possessor of property and riches, through *zakat*. Otherwise, the iniquities of greed and avarice lead to an elusive quest for luxury that further opens the door to what is called "the waste economy." As expected, illegitimate methods may also be resorted to in this senseless hunt for riches. It is these destructive contingencies that *zakat* combats and successfully eradicates.

I. ZAKAT IS A MEANS OF "DUA" (i.e. PRAYER OR GOOD WISHES)

Zakat, through various ways, acquires *dua* or good wishes for the giver. As stated in the Qur'an, it attracts the precious *dua* of the Messenger of God (upon whom be peace), not to mention the sincere wishes of the recipient. Angels join the person in offering these good wishes for the rich, from whom he has received a helping hand. The Qur'an's advice to the Prophet (upon whom be peace) is, in fact, as such: "Take alms of their wealth so that you may purify and sanctify them thereby, and pray for them for your prayers are a comfort for them" (Tawba 9:103). The Prophet's well-wishes for people desiring to offer *zakat* was, and is, renowned, as exemplified here: "O God! Treat them with Your mercy and accept their *dua*." From time to time, the Prophet personally uttered the name of a Companion, such as Abdullah ibn Awf, for whom he prayed as such: "O Lord! Have mercy on his family and accept his *duas*."[28]

To wish benefits from God upon providers of *sadaqa* or *zakat* is what comes naturally, as cursing such people is horrendously against human nature. Therefore pronouncing the wish "May God be pleased with you!" towards such people is virtually translating the feelings embedded in the heart. As noted before, the hadith, "Two angels descend each day; one of them praying 'O God! Bestow prosperity on the wealth of those who are charitable,' and the other invoking, 'O God! Destroy the wealth of the miser,'"[29] amplifies the attitude of angels during such circumstances.

J. ZAKAT IS A COMPENSATION FOR SINS

As an outcome of His unlimited mercy, God accepts good deeds as a means of granting the servant proximity with Him as well as compensation for prior sins. The Noble Prophet (upon whom be peace) has personally emphasized how acts such as ablution for prayers, the daily prescribed prayers, the Friday prayer, Ramadan fasting and even walking to the mosque compensate for sins that were committed beforehand. Indeed, *zakat* is no different, as enunciated in the Qur'an:

> God said: "I am with you; if you establish *salat* and pay the *zakat*, and believe in My Messengers and support them, and lend to God a goodly loan, surely I shall remit your sins, and surely I shall admit you into gardens beneath which rivers flow." (Maida 5:12)

The Messenger of God had made use of the subsequent words in accentuating the compensatory facet of *zakat* among other deeds: "*Salat, zakat*, enjoining good and forbidding evil is compensation for a person's shortcomings towards his/her home, family and neighbors."[30]

The Hadith "Protect yourselves from hellfire, even it be with half a date,"[31] underlines the importance of *sadaqa* and *zakat*, even if these be a tiny portion, in making amends for a person's wrongs, along with providing a shield against the torment of punishment.

K. *ZAKAT* IS SECURITY

Having expressed excruciating anxiety soon after the First Revelation, the nervousness of the Noble Prophet (upon whom be peace) was appeased by the soothing words of his wife, Khadija: "No, no…I swear, God will never forsake you; for you always visit your relatives, speak the truth, help others (physically and financially), treat your guests well and be of assistance in everything pertaining to the Truth."[32]

Abu Bakr had come across ibn Daginna, on his attempted migration to Abyssinia, who asked, "Where are you going?" Abu Bakr replied, "My tribe has tormented me, making life hell and has finally driven me out." Ibn Daginnah, a socially influential man, retorted "No way! Return, for you are a man who does righteous deeds and lends physical and financial help to others. From now on, you are under my protection."[33] All this alludes to how acts like *zakat*, *sadaqa* and giving general assistance provide the security and protection of God, as well as gaining the trust of the public.

L. *ZAKAT* LIBERATES FROM MATERIAL SLAVERY

Zakat unfetters from the shackles of excessive love for material things. Islam, in fact, insists that a person be free from all sinister fetters and turn his heart purely in the direction of God, so to speak.

For man, becoming a slave for something that he is the master of is an awful digression from the purpose of his creation. Everything has been created for mankind, who should make use of this privilege in utilizing it in the way outlined by Islam, in natural conformity with the divine will. Otherwise, this could well end in the material universe being unduly elevated to a virtual object of worship, causing a detrimental sway in feelings, thoughts and actions. The Noble Prophet (upon whom be peace) has emphasized this most unfortunate digression: "Woe to the slaves of gold, silver, linen and silk! If they are granted these, they celebrate, but they cannot digest when deprived of them."[34]

The most effective cure for this disease is, again, *zakat*, an eternal investment that is an excellent means of orienting the heart of the benefactor towards the Hereafter.

M. OTHER BENEFITS OF *ZAKAT*

So far, we have attempted to outline the immediate benefits comprised by *zakat*. By no means is this the end of it, as each emphasized point can easily be elaborated further, many possible benefits may not even have been mentioned, and there are certainly future benefits that time will unfold.

More importantly, our helplessness in the arena of expounding the aspects of *zakat* and its benefits, as these transcend our comprehension, must incessantly be kept in mind. The benefits that have not been mentioned under a separate heading, though found in other texts pertaining to *zakat*, can be encapsulated as follows: *zakat* cures illnesses,[35] shields against disasters and catastrophes,[36] grants its benefactor martyrdom,[37] and becomes torment in the afterlife for its denier.[38]

WHAT ARE THE BENEFITS OF *ZAKAT* FOR ITS RECIPIENT?

A. ZAKAT LIBERATES FROM SLAVERY TO SUSTENANCE

An addition to rescuing society from falling victim to poverty, *zakat* eliminates socially detrimental crimes like theft and robbery, as the common factor usually underlying these crimes is poverty in one way or another. Once the lack of faith, which deters from crime, is added to poverty, not much reason remains to prevent the perpetration of such crimes.

Through the promulgation of *zakat*, Islam seeks to extirpate, from the onset, social diseases like theft, by destroying their very foundation and preventing their establishment. By utilizing the privilege of performing *zakat*, the wealthy not only offer a righteous act of worship, they also soothe the poor, providing them with financial relief and thus preventing them from taking up theft as a means of sustenance. In an interesting wise, the poor receive needed recognition in the community as people sought after by the rich to allow them to complete their obligations. This, in no way, should be conceived as freeloading, as this is something unthinkable for a healthy Muslim. Rather, *zakat* is financial help during a rainy day, in a sense, encouraging the recipient to take brand new steps. Condescending to freeloading off others, for a Muslim who possesses the power to make his own ends meet, is totally unacceptable in Islam, which praises work by holding it equal with worship. For a healthy Muslim, unemployment is only temporary, and *zakat* provides the much-needed spirit and catalyst during that transitional period until the recipient becomes a giver himself.

The Noble Prophet enumerates poverty that "makes one forget the Lord"[39] among the seven things that must be avoided before their arrival. A person suffering in the throes of extreme poverty, along with many things, is bound to forget the purpose of creation. Such a ruinous thought must be avoided as it will only add to the person's sufferings by causing additional anguish in the hereafter.

B. ZAKAT HELPS ACHIEVE WORKING POWER

Zakat is a source of power for the needy. In addition to providing the financially stricken poor with desperately needed capital, *zakat* also injects in them a dynamic energy, instilling in them the confidence to provide for their own.

By hindering stockpiling, *zakat* bestows an intense vitality on the economy as well as ultimately providing matchless opportunities for the unemployed, winning them back to the community. Islam incessantly encourages individuals to be effervescently active, conversely condemning laziness and time-wasting.

Consequently, it is not difficult to imagine the enormity of the contributions to the overall economy brought by the person who is given such a great opportunity, as a result of the application of an invaluable teaching.

The prevalently unfortunate state of young people in secular societies, who squander their time and precious potential in such places as pubs and casinos, reinforces the importance of *zakat*. A country whose non-contributing masses have been revivified through such a process whereby wealth is continuously cycled for the benefit of all, will inevitably experience an economic revitalization.

C. ZAKAT PROMOTES EMPLOYMENT

Contrary to popular belief, *zakat* does not give rise to indolence; on the contrary, it encourages individuals to work. The Prophet of God strongly advised against being a "receiver," underlining the immense value of giving: "The higher hand is better than the lower."[40] The lower hand is always receiver's, regardless of who the giver is, even it be the government. However, if the government is acting as an intermediary in handing the poor what is acquired from the rich, this may be classified as an exemption from the reprimand of the above hadith. Islam strictly criticizes incessantly asking of others and fervently promotes self-acquired earnings by endowing it with multitudes of rewards, depending on the intentions of the person. The hadith additionally alludes to the vast rewards of the afterlife awaiting the almsgiver, and as expected, places him on a higher level in comparison with the receiver. It does not entirely condemn the receiver, of course, acknowledging the necessity of receiving alms when these are genuinely needed.

The Noble Messenger, for all intents and purposes, offers us the following advice, "Always be dignified. Evade the disgrace of begging either on the individual level or the national level through sincerely trying your best not to fall in such a state, and maintain your status of grace as a benefactor. Keep in mind that dependence on others is life of anxiety." This hadith also provides us a credo in international relations, giving us, individually or entirely, the crucial task of embracing a diligent attitude, hence delivering the Islamic world what it rightfully expects. Honor, dignity and superiority always belong to God, His Messengers, and the believers. Therefore believers should not come under the control or authority of unbelievers, for this undermines their dignity and superiority.[41] It has thus become evident that *zakat* vehemently encourages a self-liberation from dependence on others through the embracement of working as preeminent attitude.

D. ZAKAT AUGMENTS SELF-ESTEEM

The Qur'an, as stated, has unambiguously expounded the recipients of *zakat*, and in the process of searching and finding them, has strictly commanded the benefactor, individuals or the intermediary governments, to scrupulously avoid imparting any scorn. This renders the poor as an esteemed and sought-after part of society, as mentioned above.

It is imperative to locate and deliver *zakat* to those who are genuinely poor. The obligation of *zakat* is not one of the specified categories. In a case where a person misplaces *zakat*, wrongly assuming the recipient to fall under one of the categories, he is exempt from having to give again "correctly," because of his sincere intention. However, the best must be done to avoid such a scenario. The Companions of the Noble Prophet had first criticized a person who had given his *zakat* first to a thief, then to an adulterer and then to a rich person; they later modified their opinions knowing/hoping that any *zakat*, earnestly given with good intention, without an aim for error, would act as a cure to their problems. This accentuates the importance of conducting proper research in locating those genuinely eligible for *zakat* to facilitate the correct utilization.

Zakat saves the poor from being thrown into total oblivion, turning them into revered people who are sought after. Ultimately, as *zakat* pervasively functions throughout the community, the magnificent days of Umar ibn Abdulaziz, where finding an eligible recipient of *zakat* was in itself a difficult task, will inevitably return. In this environment, the poor will not search for the rich; instead, the rich will desperately hunt for the poor to remove an enormous weight off their shoulders, thus fostering a perennial gratitude towards the poor, who are essential to removing that load.

No doubt, the rich, immersed in a luxurious lifestyle, can otherwise quite easily become an object of grave envy for the poor as they battle daily for sustenance, overwhelmingly intensifying their feelings of abhorrence. When added to the disdainful demeanor of the rich, the abyss between rich and poor becomes insurmountably grave and culminates in an inveterate hatred for wealth, an attitude pervasive throughout many societies. The only way to overcome the abhorrence of the poor towards the rich lies in the performance of *zakat*; rich people's conceiving of the poor as friends in need will alter the poor's resentment changing negativity into gratitude over what has been granted to them by God through the donor and their appreciation of the rich for administering their rescue. The rich, concurrently, will feel compassion towards those whom they have helped so that mutual feelings of brotherhood will swiftly spread throughout the entire community, purging every remnant of conflict and turmoil.

Human nurtures an immense gratitude in the face of kindness. The Arabic proverb, *"al-insan abid al-ihsan,"* which can be translated into English as, "Man is a slave of kindness," is an expression of this profound truth. By giving *zakat*, the rich extinguish the flames of hate and envy burning in the heart of the poor, simultaneously cultivating the seeds of love and compassion—a scene that is impossible to witness wherever the rich refrain from assisting the poor. *Zakat*, in this aspect, prevents civil unrest and discord, for what perpetually lies at the root of much of today's most critical socio-economic problems is material dissatisfaction, a hegemony wherein a certain few and their chronic desire for financial domination are pitted against the frustrations of many. In that way, *zakat* performs the inimitable role of "equalizer," providing inherent stability and satisfaction for all sectors of a society, thereby engendering a more peaceful coexistence than would otherwise be possible.

WHAT ARE THE BENEFITS OF *ZAKAT* ON SOCIETY?

Zakat, with its innumerable facets, is a bond between members of society, one wherein collective harmony is dependent on individual harmony. For *zakat* explicitly creates a virtuous setting that eliminates various social problems by establishing a harmonious atmosphere for both the rich and the poor. In a nutshell, *zakat* forestalls, reduces, or eliminates social conflicts, strengthens the growth of the middle class, and obviates all of the greatest social diseases pertaining to financial issues, especially interest and money-hoarding.

A. *ZAKAT* REDUCES CLASS STRUGGLES

The establishment and maintenance of social solidarity is maximized when the gap between social classes is kept at a minimum and the voids likely to cause social conflicts are filled. In other terms, relations between the rich and the poor must not deteriorate if anarchy is to be avoided. Undoubtedly, the most important power that upholds these crucial relations between the rich and the poor is *zakat* and other principles of assistance. In societies where *zakat* ceases to exist, the precipice between the rich and the poor widens to the effect where abhorrence and hatred replace love and appreciation for the poor, and concomitantly, disdain and scorn replace compassion and charity for the rich.

Leaves of history attest to the gradual deterioration of civilizations that have opted to divide themselves into conflicting classes. Their initial happiness, a fruit of uncompromising discipline, has always been, more or less, short-lived, a prelude to their swift exit from the world stage, under the debris of their own civilization, as they have paid the ultimate price for their social injustices.

By pronouncing, "*Zakat* is the bridge of Islam"[42], the Noble Messenger amplified the importance of *zakat* in abolishing economic gaps between members of society. *Zakat* is a bridge used for passing over economic strife and when the whole community makes use of this bridge, class conflicts have the potential to become part of history. This bridge also constructs a stable middle class through which increasingly more recipients of *zakat* can become its donors and a possible clash between the rich and the poor is prevented.

B. *ZAKAT* STRENGTHENS THE MIDDLE CLASS

By the prevention of the polarization of society, Islam envisages the construction of a strong middle class. In providing an opportunity for the unemployed to embark on new business ventures, *zakat* gains them back into society, stronger than ever, instead of deserting them to become burdens of the community. The strengthening of the middle class in Islam is not encouraged just through *zakat* and *sadaqa*; in actuality, there are more precepts pertaining to this issue. For instance, when dividing booty or the spoils of war among members of society, God declares:

> That which God gives as spoil to His Messenger from the people of the townships, it is for God and His Messenger (for the State) and for the near of kin, orphans, the needy and the wayfarer so it will not become the property of the rich among you. (Hashr 59:7)

The circulation of capital solely in the hands of the rich inevitably leads to them becoming richer at the expense of the poor, who then become even more stricken. In actual fact, wealth has been created for the benefit of the whole of humanity, indiscriminately. In societies where individuals are deprived and usurped of the wealth bestowed by God, the existence of social classes is tolerated and the scorn of the rich towards the poor is sustained, riches never bring true happiness; on the contrary, financial resource easily becomes a profound source of conflict, even within families and close-knit groups. Additionally, in such societies, the poor remain in perennial anxiety in regards to attaining their sustenance whereas the rich foster a similar anxiety pertaining to the security of their wealth. The resort to dangerous alternatives can thus evolve into an option for the poor, a plight we have been so used to witnessing around the world. In contrast, *zakat* eliminates all of the illegitimate options, graciously providing the poor with an ethical way out of their strife— exhaling into the community a fresh breath of life.

C. *ZAKAT* CURES SOCIAL DISEASES

The prime hindrance of the formation of a harmonious atmosphere within societies is the existence of social classes based on wealth. It is self-evident that it is an impossibility for the poor to nurture love for the rich in a society where they are turned a blind eye on. As prevalent experience has shown, such a society is destined to become a hotbed for social conflict. The following verse corroborates this proposition:

> Spend generously for the cause of God, and do not cast yourselves into destruction by your own hands. And know that God loves the doers of good. (Baqara 2:195)

The embracement of self-centeredness, at the expense of abandoning an altruistic life with social awareness, would be tantamount to trotting dangerously, as brilliantly illustrated by the Qur'an. Throwing one's self into danger is due to deserting *infaq* or spending in the way of God and its grave outcomes that immediately come to mind, including anarchy becoming the dominant force over society that further leads to inextricable national and international complications. This dissipative demeanor of the aristocratic class, indubitably, remains the prime cause underlying anarchy. It is this shockingly irresponsible attitude of the rich, who squander astronomical amounts of money to attain luxuries in an attempt to satiate their interminable carnal desires, which causes the insurgence of crude souls, leading to anarchy and eventually turning the social welfare system upside down.

Wasteful displays as such will, no doubt, wet the appetite of the poor, inculcating in them an insurmountable feeling of hatred for the rich and perhaps, an excuse to usurp their property upon the first chance given. Obstinately abiding by the notion that enormous financial gaps between individuals do not cause an implicit or explicit upheaval is simply ignoring the realities of life.

The inveterate enmity the poor have for the rich, through *zakat*, providentially evolves into love and respect, patching up the wounds initially caused by greed and selfishness.

By responding to hate with love, the rich will attain an immense respect, and consequently the bond of fraternity throughout society will be reinforced. Those who do not spend in the way of God impede the rights of others by depriving them of what is theirs and simultaneously, wrong themselves by evading an obligation. God, indeed, dislikes wrongdoers and following such a line of action would ultimately attract the dislike of the Creator.

"Indeed God does not wrong humankind in any way; but humankind wrong themselves" (Yunus 10:44) underlines how human's worst enemy is, ironically, himself. Those who indulge in "self-oppression" by avoiding *zakat* will suffer an assault of another form of oppression. "The oppressor is the sword of God; taken revenge with and

then taken revenge of"[43] is a vital principle of social life. Thus the wealthy that are in denial of their duty with regards to alms are prone to suffering onslaughts from the poor as immediate punishment for their ignorance. The poor, given they partake in such an upheaval, are also punished in turn, as the realization of the celestial cycle enunciated by the Prophet of God. God may delay a punishment, but when His verdict is decreed, there is no turning back.

Those who furtively stockpile wealth and withhold it in fear of *zakat* are bound to receive an uncalculated slap in the face as their insatiable greed generates unavoidable calamities from their wealth.

By fixing the problem before it spreads, *zakat* forestalls the potential complications of society, establishing a firm social structure. Looking from this perspective, many current issues could be avoided if *zakat* is effectively utilized.

D. *ZAKAT* LIBERATES SOCIETY FROM INTEREST

Interest has come to be an essential method of exploitation for the happy minority in their quest for greater wealth. While attempting to establish a society where benevolence reigns, it is inevitable that an effective antidote be applied to extirpate interest, to its very last residue, to prevent the upsurge of many social predicaments.

God, the Almighty, has explicitly forbidden all types and forms of interest, the chief catalyst in causing the rich to become richer and the poor to become poorer—repudiating the common notion that interest increases wealth. The Qur'an, which had aimed to put end to the widespread use of interest and liberate the believers from its fetters, again, makes use of the principle of gradualness, which was discussed earlier:

> That which you give in usury in order that it may increase on people's property has no increase with God; but that which you give in charity, seeking God's countenance, has a manifold increase. (Rum 30:39)

Though, on the surface, wealth may seem to increase with interest, in actual fact, it fails to deliver prosperity which is, instead, promptly taken away by the Creator and replaced with gradual deterioration. *Riba,* the Arabic term for interest, holds various meanings, almost all of which are negative, like destruction and devastation; and it also refers to something that carries with itself misfortune. A sharp comparison is made above between, on the one hand, *riba* or interest that bestows the wealth perennial depreciation and, on the other, *sadaqa*, the prime inviter of prosperity. What's important is the actual prosperity bestowed by God on the riches, not the ostensible increase. Seeing that God has given this assurance, it is unthinkable for Him not to realize this assurance, and He will perpetually shower prosperity on wealth out of which *sadaqa* is given, as confirmed by a copious amount of verifications. Abandoning all forms of interest and embracing *sadaqa* is a key step towards realizing social justice.

Interest contributes to an apparent increase in wealth but this increase is nothing but a veil put over its eventual depreciation. The above verse, through comparison, implicitly alludes to how *sadaqa* generates a prosperous economy for a society, as opposed to the overall deterioration caused by interest, in the purest sense of the word.

The Qur'an, by introducing the prohibition on interest, slowly prepared the early Muslim society for the total acceptance of *zakat*, by articulating how the Jews, due to partaking in forbidden interest, were deprived of many things which were otherwise previously permissible:

> Because of the wrong-doings of the Jews, We made unlawful for them certain good things which were otherwise lawful; and because they hindered many from God's way, and of their taking usury when they were forbidden from it, and of their devouring people's wealth by wrongful means. (Nisa 4:160-1)

> O you who believe! Do not live on usury, multiplying your wealth many times over (as compound interest). Have fear of God, that perhaps you may be successful. (Al Imran 3:130)

This last revelation proved to be an unambiguous declaration, comprising serious threats for indulgers in interest:

> Those who swallow usury shall rise up (from their graves) before God like the men whom Satan has bewitched and maddened by (his) touch, for they assert that usury is just like trading, although God has permitted trade and forbidden usury. He that receives an admonition from his Lord and mends his way may keep what he has already earned; his affair will be determined by God. But those that return (to usury) will be the rightful owners of the Fire. They will abide there forever. God blights usury and makes almsgiving fruitful; He does not love the impious and the guilty. Those that believe and do good works, and establish *salat* and pay *zakat* will be rewarded by their Lord; and no fear shall come upon them, neither shall they grieve. O you who believe! Have fear of God, and give up what is still due to you from usury, if you are true believers. And if you do not, then be warned of war (against you) by God and His Messenger. If you repent you may retain your principal (without interest). Wrong not, and you shall be not wronged. And if the debtor is in straitened circumstances, then grant him a postponement until a (time of) ease; but if you remit the debt as almsgiving it will be better for you, if you did but know. (Baqara 2:275-80)

As stated above, God and His Messenger deem interest-oriented transactions as a reason to wage war, which in effect, means an exile from Divine Mercy for the rebellious perpetrators. By retorting, *"Shall I bow to him (Adam) whom You have made of clay?"* (Isra 17:61), Satan had become the first rebel through his denouncing the Divine Command. Such a seditious demeanor, therefore, is commensurable with that of Satan's who ultimately was branded with the curse and expelled from the Eternal Compassion of God.

Looking from a transactional perspective, it becomes evident that those who knowingly indulge in usury face the threat being doomed to a fate similar to that of Satan's, vis-a-vis, expulsion from the mercy of God. Insisting on dealing with interest is to come into conflict with the Creator. The result of such an action is evident: Those who are adamant in delusively claiming right over others' wealth or money will live as if struck by Satan, the very same state in which they will resurrect.

The reason for this punishment is that they iniquitously equate usury with trade, claiming its permissibility; this is a case of an incorrect perspective yielding conclusions that are immensely wide off the mark. By paying close attention to the Qur'anic instruction instead, we can gain a better insight to the very psychology that affords them this misunderstanding. In other words, by asserting that, *"Trading is just like usury"*, usurers actually dare to suggest that trading and usury are ethical equals. Yet the clear Qur'anic directive, *"God has permitted trade and forbidden usury,"* unambiguously puts an end to all possible debates. Usury and interest are an assault on property and wealth, whose protection is just as essential as the protection of life and chastity. In fact, all religions highlight, in one way or another, a person's duty to protect the five essentials of faith, mind, property, life and progeny. The hadith, "A believer's property, blood and chastity are forbidden to another believer,"[44] amplifies this outlook. In this context, usury is an attack on property from which we are compelled to protect ourselves, and a sinister means of exploiting the sweat of others. From another perspective, allowing usury to operate means the ultimate blow to production as men will preponderantly prefer to adopt methods that provide them easy earnings in their quest for satiating their natural inclination for wealth. With usury, this inclination is wastefully exploited, instead of cultivating the world, and many promising talents are laid waste on by the embracement of the motto "Invest in interest, and lay back!"

Usury, a practice that destroys *qard al-hasan*, (i.e lending money to those in need just for the sake of God, a pivotal part of the Islamic spirit) concurrently terminates the social bond, leaving each person to solve financial problems individually rather than seeking a communal help. As a result, nobody is left with a problem-free opportunity to borrow money. *Qard al-hasan*, a vehemently emphasized facet of Islam, is given eighteen times more reward than *sadaqa*.[45] This precious practice reinforces the belief that whatever the expected surplus is, it should strictly be expected from God.

Together with forbidding participation in sin and enmity, the Qur'an strongly encourages virtue and goodness[46] as the principal causes of action, whether it is good or bad, necessarily attracts the same degree of responsibility.

Simply put, the acceptance of usury in public life means siding with the rich and immorally leaving the poor to fight their own desperate battle. This, indeed, represents complete deviation from Divine Mercy and Compassion. Although God grants wealth to the rich, He also provides a sanctuary for the poor through decreeing alms and charity.

And yet, the vices of usury are not limited to what has already been mentioned. Perhaps the ultimate motive should be sought in a more profound domain. What is important is that the Creator has sternly forbidden usury and has given permission for trading. In reality, the key factor that paves our direction is the simple commands or prohibitions of God, not the entailing beneficial results that surface upon their application. Therefore, the benefits are subordinate to our efforts and striving to achieve the blessing of the Almighty, through abhorring what has been decreed as being abhorrent, and embracing what has been decreed as being worthy of embrace.

Sadaqa, an initiator of blessings and prosperity with all its types, is also the golden key to the copious treasures of Divine Compassion. By virtue of a miraculous style of articulation, the Qur'an illustrates charity as an act that brings the provider closer to God, so to speak; incorporates him or her into Paradise; reinforces the spiritual bond between believers and humankind in general; and takes the provider far away from Satan and hellfire, as opposed to amplifying the numerous harms inherent in interest. Such harms, whenever and wherever they are incurred, become a motive or means for distancing one's self from the Compassion of the Creator and from the entrance into Paradise; for coming closer to Satan and the hellfire; and for erecting insidious walls between people.

The Qur'anic declaration *"God blights usury and makes almsgiving fruitful,"* at once destroys the possibility of exploiting others' earnings through usury, a practice which aims to demolish the very foundation of social justice; one could say that it provides a cure for a disease before it takes hold of the whole body. The realization of this cure is through an uncompromising establishment of the institutions for alms and charity, and forever shutting the door on iniquitable practices whose menacing effects are extensively renowned. The number of investors whose dreams of riches and luxury have become horrendous nightmares through the manipulations of interest are by no means few. Opposed to these, there are countless souls whose wealth has multiplied in great magnitudes thanks to *sadaqa*, not to mention the love they have earned from the masses. By now, it should be blatantly evident that usury is a destroyer of social balance and a spoiler of the mutual harmony which is the unbending backbone of human life.

Not coincidentally, this verse relating to usury is among the final revelations of the Qur'an; its prohibition was declared during the concluding days of the Prophet's (upon whom be peace) life. The Messenger of God, during the Farewell Pilgrimage, put the prohibition of usury into effect, first by abolishing his uncle Abbas's interest, thereby setting a perfect example. Throughout those sermons, addressed somewhat as farewells to his Companions, he abolished blood feuds and then pronounced, "Beware! All previous usury is now under my feet, and the first interest I abolish is that of Abbas ibn Abdul Muttalib."[47] Absolutely nobody hesitated, including Abbas, in abandoning their anticipated hoards of interest; moreover, they started agonizing over possible divine penalties for their prior indulgence in usury. A soothing edict, however, was revealed soon after, dispersing the noble Companions' anxiety:

> There is no sin on those who believe and do good, righteous deeds for what they might have partaken (in the past), provided (henceforth) they fear (the end of their previous creeds and misdeeds) and come to faith and do good, righteout deeds, then keep from disobedience to God in reverence for Him and piety and believe (more profoundly), then be more meticulous in obeying God in greater reverence for Him and piety and be devoted to doing good, aware that God is seeing them. (Maida 5:93)

Belief and sincerity have been reiterated three times in the above verse. This reinforces the importance of abstaining from the forbidden for protection from the hellfire, and in turn, the value of refraining from doubtful cases in order to avoid falling into the domain of the forbidden, thereby causing the inner self to decay. The the Noble Prophet declared, "Leave what gives you doubt, stick to what is certain."[48] In another hadith that follows a similar trait, the Messenger has evidently stated that the *halal* (i.e. permissible) and the *haram* (i.e. non-permissible) have unequivocally become clear; thus the doubtful must be evaded, a recommended course of action that places emphasis on one's spiritual life.

An implicit illustration is also to be found through a brilliant depiction of the perennial indolence of usurers and the consequential anxieties of their parasitical lives. Those who lead such a life suffer a similar ending, facing a fitting penalty for their unjust insistence that usury constitutes normal trade. According to the interpretations of Ibn Abbas, an illustrious Companion, usurers will be resurrected in a state of strangulation. The words articulated by the Messenger of God illustrate a symbolic scene he witnessed during the *Miraj*, or Ascension, and offers us an enlightenment: "Then I saw a group whose bellies were like houses and who happened to be on the path which the Pharaoh and his folk were taken to hellfire day and night. Each time they saw Pharaoh and his folk, they would leap forward from repulsion, only to fall down face-first from the weight caused by their stomach, after which the Pharaoh and his folk would start trampling on them. I asked 'O Jibril? Who are they?' and he replied 'They are usurers.'"[49]

In another similar hadith, the Prophet mentions having seeing a group comprised of people who would fall down face first every time they attempted to get up; thus he was again informed they were usurers.[50]

This destiny is the final result of obstinately insisting on a satanic path. The Messenger of God clearly pronounced that the curse of God will indiscriminately afflict the indulgers of usury,[51] including the provider, the acceptor, the witness, the proxy, the secretary and whoever takes active part in such a dealing,[52] the doomed outcome of impudently declaring war on God and His Messenger. In fact, the fate of the entire group—the instigators and his or her various supports—is captured perfectly in a very short and powerful chapter near the conclusion of the Qur'an: *"Perish the hands of the Father of Flame! Perish he! No profit to him from all his wealth, and all his gains! Burnt soon will he be in a Fire of Blazing Flame! His wife shall carry the (crackling) wood - As fuel! A twisted rope of palm-leaf fibre round her (own) neck!"* (Tabbat 111:1-5) May God protect us all from such a destiny.

Addressing the giant mass gathered around him eighty days prior to his eternal migration from Earth, the Messenger of God pronounced that God had now perfected the religion and finalized His blessings on the Muslims, stressing that the only way to procure the blessing of God is through Islam, the submission to the will of God.

Thus, the Prophet encapsulated the basic tenets of the Qur'an, the miraculous guide for those in possession of a magnanimous spirit, as magnanimousness is perhaps the most ideal word to describe the precious state of mind of the believers who successfully eschewed usury and adopted *zakat*. In fact, the Companions who had, at that time, gained utmost maturity after a 23-year period of stringent development unconditionally surrendered to those exquisite tenets. This, in turn, underlines the significance of corrective maturity before the embracement of the principles required to annul immorality. Even though societies may achieve a head-spinning development in technology, for example, or an apparent increase in welfare through solutions to minor economic problems, no matter how happy they seem on the surface, their life-spans will never realize their full potential and they will be utterly helpless, in an imminent shake of social upheaval, as long as they carry on the practice of usury that is so fundamentally contrary to human nature. In effect, systems that move us against the tide of righteousness are no more than "sparks in the pan" and cannot provide a long-lasting illumination.

The Qur'an eloquently states, *"God invites to the Abode of Peace, and guides whom He wills to a straight path"* (Yunus 10:25). As certified by the Qur'an, the prohibition of usury was personally elaborated by the Prophet (upon whom be peace) and then additionally, he commissioned Abu Bakr and Ali to explain the prohibition accordingly to hinder possible misunderstandings. If humanity carries the serious intention of curing itself from the leech-like effects of usury, it inevitably must wake up in the illuminative realm of *iman*, belief in God, and lend an ear to the commands and prohibitions of the Almighty Creator. Observing morality in financial transactions is a virtue of believers. Thus, in a society of believers, it becomes necessary to establish alternative systems where all exploitable loopholes are firmly covered, and whereby charity-oriented institutions become established, rescuing the poor from the throes of despair.

In a nutshell, *zakat* and interest are two opposite and dichotomous poles. While *zakat* is aimed towards acknowledging the rights of the poor and eliminating obstacles that impede these rights, the essential crux of interest entails the rich ignominiously becoming richer, leaving the poor stranded in destitution. Contrary to such a devastating outcome, by preventing the exploitation of the poor, Islam also shows the rich alternative ways to make use of their wealth, free of fear and anxiety. The application of *zakat* ultimately means the extirpation of usury, endowing the society with genuine, long-lasting bliss.

E. The Other Social Benefits of *Zakat*

Indubitably, the benefits of *zakat* do not end there. Among the other benefits of *zakat* are that it is a social insurance on public life, an aura maintaining tolerance between social groups, a catalyst that puts fire in the economic life and a balancing factor that emphasizes both the importance of worldly earnings and the eternal importance of life in the eternal abode.

Each aspect which has been delineated above, as one may guess, is also a positive step towards building an unshakeable social structure. Moreover, the totality constitutes a prelude to other innumerable benefits that will arise through the utilization of *zakat*—benefits both seen and unseen, in this world and the next. God, the Exalted, is remote from indulging in any activity void of meaning and distant from negated attributes: *"Not for (idle) sport did We create the heavens and the earth and all that is between!"* (Anbiya 21:16) Therefore if *zakat* has been decreed by Him, then it unquestionably must contain a copious load of purposes, all of which will unravel in time.

CHAPTER 3

Possessions That Are Subject to *Zakat*

WHICH POSSESSIONS ARE SUBJECT TO *ZAKAT*?

T he issue of trying to determine how much *zakat* needs to be spared from a certain item, and leveling what proportion, are all predicated upon the Qur'an and Sunna. Despite the Qur'an's ardent emphasis on *zakat*, it has no specific pronouncement on the amount of *nisab*, which has been, in turn, explained by the Prophet (upon whom be peace).

The possessions subject to *zakat* can basically be encapsulated as livestock, moveable and immoveable assets, mines, agricultural harvests and commercial merchandise, all of which have different limits and amounts for *nisab*. In brief, the *nisab* for each item and the amount of *zakat* that needs to be spared from the item vary according to the item's status. "One-fortieth" has generally been a pervasive measure among public, although this calculation only pertains to commercial merchandise and sheep. Thus minerals, mines, agricultural harvests and various livestock all have been assigned various amounts and proportions of *nisab*.

A. HOW IS *ZAKAT* GIVEN ON MOVEABLE GOODS?

1. The zakat on gold and silver

Gold and silver, valuable assets in commercial life as items of jewelry, also cater to the ornamental needs of certain individuals, though it is forbidden for men to use gold jewelry. Regardless of commercial or ornamental utilization, those in possession of a *nisab's* worth of gold or silver are required to pay its *zakat*, as attested to by the Qur'an:

O you who believe! Indeed many of the rabbis and priests
devour the wealth of people by false means and debar them
from the way of God. Those who hoard up gold and silver and
do not spend it in the way of God, give tidings unto them of a
painful punishment. The day shall come when their treasures
shall be heated in hellfire; and their foreheads, sides and backs
shall be branded with them (saying), "Here is that treasure that
you hoarded up for yourselves; taste, now what you were
hoarding up." (Tawba 9:34-5)

In similar fashion, the Messenger of God has provided the following illustration: "There is no wealthy withholding the *zakat* of
the gold and silver that will not have these possessions brought to
them in the Day of Judgment, in the form of burning panels, additionally heated in the hellfire, branding their sides, foreheads and backs.
Each time these panels cool down, they will be reheated to return
the torment, until the end of judgment, in a day equivalent to fifty
thousand days. Then they will be shown the way, either to Paradise
or to Hell."[1]

As it is known, gold and silver were the currencies in circulation during the era of the Noble Messenger and the ensuing cen-
turies, evaluated as both nuggets and jewelry. Even though, in this day
and age, they are predominantly no longer utilized as currencies,
they still occupy an undoubtedly important place as economic
investments, which can be changed into currency with ease if the
need arises. Moreover, their current use as jewelry is quite pervasive
throughout society. Irrespective of the intention one has in possessing such goods, one is compelled to pay *zakat* on them once they
have accumulated to a certain level.

Various figures exist in relation to the definition of a *nisab* of
gold and silver, stemming from diverse interpretations of the meas-
urements used during the time of the Prophet (upon whom be peace)
in different areas, or simply put, according to traditional norms. The
nisab of gold, however, has generally been identified as 85 grams and
that of silver as 595 grams. According to a narration of Abu Said
al-Hudri, the Messenger of God stated that *zakat* is not required for

silver less than 5 *uqiyya*'s (200 *dirhams*=595 grams).[2] Anas ibn Malik, an official *zakat* collector during the era of Caliph Umar, asserted that he had been instructed to take ½ a dinar from every 20 dinars, a practice similar to that later followed by Caliph Ali.[3]

Taking the hadith and subsequent applications of the Companions into consideration, scholars have unanimously pinpointed the *nisab* of gold and silver as being 85 grams and 595 grams respectively, with an overall proportion of 2.5%.

2. The zakat on cash, checks and bonds

The banknotes in circulation today do not essentially possess value; rather they are simply papers assigned a nominal value. Though from the purely physical aspect they hold no resemblance to the gold and silver used during the time of the Prophet, they perform the same function. To be more precise, banknotes or cash have taken the place of gold and silver in commercial transactions. Thus, it is only logical that cash be evaluated according to the role it plays in trade; therefore, it is also integrated into the calculation of *zakat*, with a 2.5% ratio. Thus, a person in possession of checks or bonds equivalent to at least 595 grams of silver or 85 grams of gold must offer 2.5% of it as *zakat*, owing to the fact that nowadays, these have become the standard for the exchange of goods, as well as a potential means for buying.

3. The zakat on shares or investments

The practice of selling shares, propounded by companies within great investments to spread the capital among a large base and to incorporate into the commercial life the contribution of a multitude of people, can be assessed in two forms. The first denotes the capital invested during the beginning phase of a company; and the second indicates the investments that exist in the company as property or wealth.

Pertaining to the first type that involves investments in the foundation, the building and machinery, Hanafi scholars nurture a reluctant attitude in regards to subjecting it to *zakat* given that the investments end there. The Majalla Committee, organized by the Ottomans in the 19th century to systematically complete an official Islamic Code of law, nonetheless inclined towards the Malikis and opted in favor of giving *zakat* in such a situation, a verdict perhaps more fitting in terms of disseminating vigor in an otherwise dead investment. The investments within the company, on the other hand, must be assessed as commercial merchandise, with a 2.5% ratio of *zakat*, in that they can also be cashed in if required.

4. The zakat on jewelry

Even though other schools hold diverse views, the Hanafi scholars insist that *zakat* is imperative for jewelry equal to *nisab*. Thus, a woman possessing jewelry worth at least 85 grams of gold is compelled with the payment of *zakat*. Despite the fact that wearing necklaces, bracelets, earrings and other jewels are permissible for women, the Messenger of God had nurtured a profound sensitivity towards his family as far as this issue was concerned, to the effect that once, having seen his beloved daughter Fatima wearing a bracelet acquired as part of gains of war allocated for her share, he admonished her by warning, "Would you like people to say the daughter of the Prophet is fashioning a loop of hellfire around her wrist?" Having heard this, Fatima, so sensitively compassionate, hurriedly sold the bracelet and freed a slave with its money. After explaining what she did to her exceptional father, he displayed his joy by uttering, "Praise be to God who has spared the Prophet's daughter from hellfire."[4]

Insofar as Islamic Law is concerned, the wife is financially independent from her husband; in other words, a wife can possess both moveable and unmovable assets. If these assets surpass the amount of *nisab*, then according to Islam, she is considered to be rich; thus she naturally becomes obliged with the duties of the rich.

Goods owned with marriage, however, should be evaluated within the framework of the husband-wife partnership. At times, according to customary practices, the wife may be the official owner of assets and the user of jewelry, although the rights of disposition may be with the husband. In these kinds of scenarios, the husband exercises extensive rights over property. If so, then the *zakat* of these assets is counted among the husband's possessions in ascertaining the *nisab*, hence the *zakat* for both of them becomes an obligation on the husband.

Owing to the fact that the Messenger of God did not disclose any instructions in relation to jewels in particular, the jurists have maintained that no *zakat* needs to be given for pearls, diamonds, sapphires, corals and other precious stones worn by women as ornaments. We must stop here, however, and gain a more profound understanding of this issue. Does this verdict mean that the person is not responsible for paying *zakat* on these items, or need not pay it; or, does it open the possibility that it is best, and advisable, to give *zakat* on these? This, in entirety, certainly calls for reflection and contemplation.

In summary, returning back to the jurisprudential verdicts, *zakat* basically must be given of jewelry equivalent to *nisab*. If the jewelry is used for trade, then it becomes classified under commercial merchandise and is calculated accordingly. Precious stones, then, are subject to a 2.5% ratio of *zakat* given that they are utilized as commercial merchandise. On the whole, it is more appropriate to offer *zakat* even if they are being kept as items of jewelry, as the Almighty will not interrogate a person on account of giving *zakat*, but will do so in the reverse situation—and one's situation, at that point, will be irreversible.

Thus, it is more prudent to treat jewels and precious stones similarly to other jewelry like gold and silver. This recommendation is strengthened by that fact that these stones essentially have innate value and exempting them from *zakat* would open the door for stowing treasure, an iniquity denounced in both the Qur'an and Sunna.

5. The zakat on collections

In this day and age, as a result of personal interest or commercial pre-texts, the collection of various items has become a pervasive practice. In some instances, they can even gain astronomical values which are difficult to estimate.

Looking from the perspective of the Qur'an and Sunna, no clear-cut verdict can be cited. Like in most other issues, however, a sound decision can be reached predicated upon general principles of Islam and extrapolations from similar situations. Thus, if the items are collected with commercial intention, then the verdict is evident; the collection is subject to a 2.5% *zakat*. However, if collecting is practised as a hobby or a pasttime, then it ought to be regarded as *kanz* (i.e. stowed treasure), whereby it again becomes subject to a 2.5% *zakat*. Adopting this approach effectively disperses all excuses to evade paying *zakat* and renders an advantage when considering the *sadd al-dharayi* principle in Islamic law, which elaborates the necessity of blocking all roads that lead to iniquity. In effect, collectables, some of which may even have gained a worldwide market, can easily be sold and cashed-in at any given time. Requiring *zakat* for these effectively prevents people from collecting simply as a pretext to avoid paying *zakat*.

6. The zakat on additional accessories

Except for basic necessities, *zakat* is required for additional accessories and clothing that are kept at home. This demands first the identification of these extras, and second, the integration of these items into the calculation of *zakat*. These "additional items" include all sorts of clothes, equipment and household devices and appliances that cannot be considered an absolute necessity. Consequently, it would be wise to reassess the whole contents of the house prior to offering *zakat*.

B. How is *ZAKAT* given on unmovable assets?

The system of *zakat*, promulgated by Islam not just for moveable assets but to cover all areas of possible investment, is an absolute social solution. By unmovable assets, we mean all types of real estate that a person owns (e.g. houses, land, hotels, factory buildings etc). It proficiently sets forth the necessity in paying alms for unmovable assets encompassing billions of dollars worth of commercial ventures. According to the Hanafi School, *zakat* must be given from the revenues of assets, other than those which are basic necessities, like houses, businesses, apartments, and so on. The Maliki School, conversely, maintains that the *zakat* should be extracted out of the asset itself, a verdict in concordance with the decision of the Majalla Committee, despite the differing opinion of Hanafi scholars. The Majalla Committee reached this conclusion considering, sympathetically, the benefits to Muslims in general, and by taking into account the *masalih al-mursal* principle of Islamic Law—that is, the existence of one or another enormous advantage which is inherent in deciding upon a certain verdict. From a contemporary perspective, this verdict seems quite appropriate, as the preponderant pretext for investing in unmovable assets, these days, is for "commercial use." Thus, inevitably, the commercial holdings must themselves be subject to *zakat*.

We can perhaps clarify the issue further by looking at it from two separate perspectives. Unmovable assets are generally either agricultural/commercial land or real estate. If it is agricultural land, then it is evident; depending on the nature of the effort required to maintain it, a one-tenth or one-twentieth ratio of *ushr* from the produce is paid while the asset itself does not become subject to *zakat*. However, if the land in question is not being used for agricultural purposes, or if there is no crop growing for more than three years, the rights of use need to be handed over to somebody else who will make agricultural use of it, as it is evident that the current land-holder is, in fact, not in need of the land. If, on the other hand, the land-holder then claims that the land had been bought to fulfill commercial purposes, he would be obliged to pay its *zakat* using the standard 2.5% ration—for example, $2500 on land worth $100,000. The case for real estate is not much different. A person owning additional houses apart from the one in which he lives in must follow suit. As indicated by the Majalla Committee, the *zakat* on the building must be calculated based on its current value. Suggesting otherwise, for instance that *zakat* ought to be calculated based on the estate's rent instead, or only, would be tantamount to impeding on the rights of alms recipients. For instance, although amounts will surely differ from one place to another, let's assume the total rent per annum on a $100,000 house to be approximately $6000. Paying *zakat* from the rent results in a calculation of $150 only, in contrast to the $2500 worth of *zakat* extracted from the house itself.

Scrutinizing the issue from another viewpoint, it becomes blatantly clear that virtually no one, in the current world, buys a second house simply to benefit from its rent; rather, real estate is perceived as an investment that reaps both current and future revenues. Therefore, it is only natural that real estate investments be treated as commercial commodities.

According to these preceding factors, and in harmony with the spirit of *zakat*, it is undoubtedly more appropriate to follow the Maliki School and the Majalla Committee on this issue. As well as being in harmony with Islamic ideals, this verdict also secures better benefits for the poor. Bearing in mind that the needs of the poor, destitute, students, and the Muslim public in general are taken care of with the money acquired through *zakat*, nobody has the prerogative to hinder or impede such a socially beneficial system. And, most importantly, God will bestow a multitude of rewards on those, according to their intentions, who sacrifice their wealth throughout all times of need.

C. HOW IS *ZAKAT* GIVEN ON COMMERCIAL MERCHANDISE?

The Qur'an describes the process of giving *zakat* of commercial commodities as an obligation for believers. A verse relating to this articulates, *"O you who believe! Spend of the good things which you have earned, and of that which We have brought out of the earth for you"* (Baqara 2:267). Samurrah ibn Jundab, one of the Companions of the

Noble Messenger, has also clearly testified in support of the prophetic command of *zakat* being required on commercial merchandise.[5]

All items subject to trade, such as tools, machinery, food items, clothing, animals, jewelry, land, and real estate, effectively, are regarded as commercial merchandise and thus are directly subject to *zakat*. For an item or a property to be classified as commercial merchandise, however, it must necessarily be kept with the intention of acquiring revenue or profit from it; and in addition, it must be offered in trade. Critically, therefore, a person holding the intention of making commercial use of possessions obtained through donations, wills, or inheritance must include those possessions when calculating his overall *zakat*, since according to the Hanafi Scholar Abu Yusuf, they have effectively become commercial merchandise owing to personal intention. Looking at it from this perspective, the rent acquired from a car, house or land must also be deemed as a commercial commodity.

As for the *nisab* on commercial commodities, they have been identified as 85 grams of gold or 595 grams of silver. Regardless of possible fluctuations throughout the year, the *nisab* must be equivalent to the above amounts both at the start and end of the year. Importantly, these items subject to *zakat* are evaluated at the end of the year, each according to their market value, irrespective of prior fluctuations. The apparent end-of-the-year value is taken into consideration, as opposed to the selling price or other customary standards, given that the sale has actually not taken place.

The stipulation of "an elapse of a year" just mentioned as a necessary requirement for such possessions to become subject to *zakat* does not become invalid if or when, throughout the year, certain items are exchanged with other items of the same or different nature or value. For instance, if a trader sold the construction steel he owned at the start of the year and bought carpets instead, which he then again sold and entered into the brick industry, he is still obliged with *zakat* given that his overall possessions exceed the *nisab*.

Livestock or other animals which are fed for commercial purposes are also considered as commercial merchandise and subject to 2.5% *zakat*. These possessions themselves can be presented as *zakat*;

or, the 2.5% value on these possessions may be calculated and given in cash.

In summary, in light of this information, a trader would calculate, in cash value, his entire commercial possessions, and then offer a 2.5% *zakat* of the calculated aggregate, including the money lent and the money expected from unpaid sales, excluding his debts.

D. HOW IS *ZAKAT* GIVEN ON MOTOR VEHICLES?

Included in a person's basic necessities, in addition to a house, household items, clothes and food, are vehicles of transport. From this point of view, it initially becomes evident that no *zakat* is required on motor vehicles. As in the case of houses and household items, however, opting to fulfill this necessity luxuriously, which could have otherwise be fulfilled—owning cars which carry astronomical price tags—alters the prior viewpoint. In such cases, *zakat* comes into the picture, as these can no longer be considered to be simply items of necessity, owing to their pomposity. Notwithstanding the argument of some that people necessarily should own vehicles appropriate with their social positions, offering *zakat* on these vehicles certainly stands as a more prudent approach. Such a course of action implies forestalling, from the outset, possible dissent against wealth, and in fact, only by virtue of this approach will the social benefits of *zakat* be procured.

Thus, on one hand, no barriers are placed in front of those desiring expensive cars; while on the other, the possible ill feelings of the poor towards the rich are purged right from the beginning. And, as always, the morality of *zakat* comes into focus as man, essentially, makes his calculation of what is payable in the all-encompassing gaze of God.

In a case where vehicles are owned for trade or profit, the situation is entirely different and a simple calculation of one-fortieth, 2.5%, *zakat* is required on their total revenue. Taxis, buses, commercial trucks, interstate coaches, and so on, can be classified under this group. Even the value of number plates on taxis and minibuses, in some cities, can reach 10 or 20 times the value of the vehicle itself, which, in turn, reflects on the earned revenue. The revenue on trucks and semi-trailers used for transporting goods is also subject to *zakat*, and in similar vain, that of sea or air transportation vehicles. Vehicles used within a company, factory, or building site, such as forklifts and cranes, are classified as commercial machinery and also subject to *zakat* using the standard calculation.

In a nutshell, the *zakat* on vehicles owned for personal use is calculated according to its overall value, whereas the *zakat* on commercial vehicles is calculated according to its revenue.

E. HOW IS *ZAKAT* GIVEN ON LIVESTOCK?

As the *nisab* and ratio of *zakat* differ according to the item, as discussed above, so it also varies depending on the type and age of an animal held as livestock. In fact, camels, sheep and cattle all have independent systems for the calculation of *zakat*, all of which the Prophet himself (upon whom be peace) unambiguously designated.

1. The zakat on camels

Camels, as known, belong to desert climates and therefore may not be found in most of the geographical areas of the world. In many Muslim countries, however, they still undoubtedly hold significance as livestock with numerous benefits. The era of the Noble Prophet was a time when camels enjoyed immense popularity as virtually inseparable instruments of social life, ultimately holding a very profound meaning for the people of the region, utilized for riding, as beasts of burden, and as sources of meat and milk.

Moreover, camels at that time were a testament to the financial strength of a person. As understood by the grievous testimony of Kab ibn Malik, divulging his regret from lagging behind during the preliminary preparations for the Tabuk campaign, owning two camels was then considered to be a sign of wealth.[6]

Camels, in places maintaining their widespread use, still connote economic power, thus the validity of their subjection to *zakat* remains. The Islamic verdict pertaining to the *zakat* on camels has been ascertained, predicated upon the narrations of Anas ibn Malik, who describes his official correspondence with Caliph Abu Bakr in relation to the *zakat* on camels, to the effect that the former was given the following written instructions by the Caliph, embossed with the seal of the Prophet:

> When one has 5 grazing camels for one year, their due is 1 sheep, which is also the due for 5 to 9 camels. The due for 10 to 14 camels is 2 sheep; for 15 to 19 camels it is 3 sheep; and for 20 to 24 camels it is 4 sheep. The due for 25 to 35 camels is a 2-year-old she-camel; for 36 to 45 it is a 3-year-old she-camel; for 46 to 60 it is a 4-year-old she-camel; for 61 to 75 it is a 5-year-old she-camel; for 76 to 90 it is two 3-year-old she-camels; and for 91 to 120 it is two 5-year-old she-camels.[7]

2. The zakat on cattle

The *zakat* required on cattle, another key multipurpose animal, has again been explicitly identified by hadith. Oxen, too, are classified under the same category. The measure instructed by the Noble Messenger pertaining to the *nisab* and amount of compulsory *zakat* on cattle are as follows:

> The nisab for cattle is 30. For 30 to 40 heads of cattle, a 2.5 year-old male or female weaned calf; for 40 to 60, a 3 year-old weaned calf; for 60, two 1 year-old calves. For more than 60 heads of cattle, the rate is one calf per 30 heads and 1 weaned calf per 40 heads.[8]

These measures are for those who own cattle for other than commercial reasons. Those who buy and sell cattle, however, are obliged with a 2.5% zakat, as is the case with other commercial goods. Precisely, whenever a commodity sways towards a commercial domain, insofar as *zakat* is concerned, it is considered as commercial merchandise and thus subject to the standard of 2.5% *zakat*.

3. The zakat on sheep

The Prophet (upon whom be peace) has explained the necessary amount of *zakat* and *nisab* required on sheep. The instructions found in a treatise dictated by the Messenger to the *zakat* collectors regarding the *zakat* of sheep, can briefly be encapsulated as follows:

> When one has 40 sheep or goats, their due is 1 sheep, which is the same for 40 to 120 sheep or goats. For 120 to 200 sheep, it is 2 sheep; for 200 to 399 it is 3 sheep; and for 400 to 500 it is 4 sheep.[9]

4. The zakat on horses and similar animals

Man's purpose in keeping horses varies greatly, and whether they are subject to *zakat* or not differs according to these variances. During earlier times when horses were used in warfare, they could not be subject to *zakat*, simply because they were classified as war equipment, in line with the Prophet's declaration, "*zakat* is not required of a Muslim's horse or slave."[10]

Today, horses are certainly kept for reasons other than warfare—namely, for riding or transporting heavy loads—sometimes even strictly for racing, not for gambling but for pleasure. On the word of Abu Hanifa horses are subject to *zakat*, a verdict predicated upon the hadith transmitted by Zayd ibn Thabit: "One *dinar* or ten *dirham*s for every horse in possession that roams freely."[11] Accordingly, the owner has the free choice of either paying in cash for each horse, whether it is male or female, or treating it as a commercial possession, and thus extracting a one-fortieth amount of *zakat*. But keeping the horses for commercial intentions, would classify them as commercial merchandise, effectively nullifies the previous free choice.

Donkeys and mules that are exempt from *zakat* become subject to it when they are possessed for purposes of trade.

Perhaps the most important factor that distinguishes horses from other livestock is that they do not provide benefits from their meat, milk or wool. Hence, what remains important in horses is reproduction, whereas *nama* (augmentation), an imperative prerequisite of *zakat*, is the most central characteristic of other livestock. For that reason, horses are rarely kept by a single owner for purposes other than breeding, essentially a pretext for trade, and in line with this intention, they thus become subject to *zakat*.

5. The zakat on other animals

In addition to the animals for which *zakat* has evidently been elucidated by revelation, there are also those that have not been given a mention. Rapid industrial development has begotten countless new sectors, many of which are founded on animal breeding. Today in various regions of the world, animals or livestock are fed with the intention of benefiting from their products, like bees for honey, cows and sheep for milk, chickens for eggs, silkworms for silk etc…In fact, a great amount of production takes place in established modern dairies, poultry farms, trout-farms, and places built for beekeeping and sericulture. A question that may naturally come to mind regarding the *zakat* on these animals would be answered by stating that a 2.5% *zakat* is necessitated, in that they constitute commercial merchandise. In other words, if they are kept for commercial intentions, a 2.5% *zakat* is required; but if, on the contrary, they are fed for personal needs, then their *zakat* and *nisab* are evident. In essence, then, these animals become subject to *zakat* once they enter the commercial domain. This is the general principle which is applicable to any animal or insect.

F. HOW IS *ZAKAT* GIVEN ON ANIMAL PRODUCTS?

Apart from what has been stated above, we must determine whether the revenue acquired from the products of these animals should be integrated into the *zakat* calculations. However, if one compares the animals to factory machinery and tools, one might conclude that only the product would be subject to *zakat*. It is imperative, then, that these issues, which increasingly arise amid the changing times, be continually reassessed from the viewpoint of *zakat*—always with the intention of pleasing God and honoring the noble goals of *zakat*.

As for the *zakat* on honey, Maliki and Shafii scholars maintain that *zakat* is not necessary owing to its resemblance to milk in terms of its liquid texture, and due to the lack of sound evidence in relation to honey. Yet, in the view of Hanafi and Hanbali scholars, honey entails a *zakat* of one-twentieth, or an amount of *ushr*, namely one-tenth. The Hanafi scholars have not set a restraint on the *nisab* of honey, in contrast to the Hanbali scholars who have identified it as 10 *faraqs* (100 grams) thereof, substantiating this judgment with a few hadith and with the practice of the the four pious caliphs who succeeded the Prophet (upon whom be peace) and the succeeding times.

In a hadith conveyed by Ibn Umar, the Messenger of God pronounces, "For every ten measures of honey, one is for *zakat*,"[12] a point similarly stressed on another account, "one water-skin for every ten," transmitted by Amr ibn Shuayb.[13]

When Abu Sayyara came to the Prophet and said, "O Messenger of God! I own bees," the Prophet responded, "Then you must pay their *ushr*."[14]

Embarking off from these and other similar evidence, Abu Hanifa decided on the necessity of *ushr* or one-tenth for honey acquired from lands exempt from *kharaj* i.e. a special tax imposed on the yield of the land, and effectively, this is the view embraced by the Hanafi school.

G. HOW IS *ZAKAT* PAID ON AGRICULTURAL PRODUCTS?

Ushr, the term given to the *zakat* of harvest obtained from land through cultivation—a practice, in our day, that has sadly almost fallen into disrepute—encompasses various assessments depending on the status of the land and the energy committed to acquiring the harvest. On this subject, the Qur'an announces general principles that consequently enjoin *zakat* on agricultural crops, such as:

> O you who believe! Spend of the good things which you have earned, and of that of which We have brought out of the earth for you. (Baqara 2:267)

> Eat of the fruit thereof when they are in season, and pay the
> due thereof upon the harvest day. (An'am 6:141)

In connection with the topic, the Noble Messenger has proclaimed clearly, "There is an *ushr* on crops that grow by rainwater, streams or by themselves through absorbing water into their roots, and half an *ushr* on irrigated crops."[15]

Including a slight difference in minor details, all schools are in agreement that crops grown effortlessly require a *zakat* of one-tenth and those grown with greater effort entail a *zakat* of one-twentieth.

The Hanafi school, by virtue of taking into consideration the generalization of the judgments within the verse, have laid down that *ushr* can be acquired of all kinds of agricultural harvest, contrary to the opinion of Muhammad ibn Idris al-Shafii, who suggests that crops that are able to be stored for a long time are subject to *zakat*. The Maliki and Hanbali schools, almost in line with the Hanafi scholars, maintain that agricultural crops should all be considered for *ushr*.

Evidently, the Hanafi school handles this issue in a more extensive manner, whereupon crops that have become significant sources of income in many countries such as cotton, linen, sugarcane and so on, are effectively included in the process of *ushr* collection, thus expediently balancing the number of rich and poor in society. In some jurisprudential books, there has recently been a mention of virtually ushr-free crown land (*miri* land), a blatant mistake that must be corrected. From a historical perspective, from the very beginning of the Ottoman Empire to its collapse, for instance, the Sultan—not the public—paid tax, or ushr, on the land he owned. Thus, in some books, the terms *Arazi al-Amriyya* or *Arazi al-Sultaniyya* have been abbreviated as *Arazi al-Miri* (chief's land or the Sultan's land), according to which the rulings have been predicated upon.

At various times throughout history, in fact, land reforms have been carried out whereby each land has gradually become privatized. The new land-owners, previously not obliged with the payment of *ushr* on this land, had now become responsible for it as they took proprietorship from the crown. Today, the definition and responsibilities of ownership have become clearly delineated to the effect that even when a government wishes to expropriate land, it first must purchase the title deed. For this reason, the new and disturbing rulings mentioned in above, which are found in a limited number of books of jurisprudence, must be carefully reassessed, for there is strong unanimity in the whole Islamic world regarding the necessity of ushr.

H. How is *ZAKAT* given on mines and minerals?

The word *madan* (mine) has two separate connotations in the Arabic language: *Kanz* and *rikaz*. *Kanz* practically means all things like treasure, fortune, relics and antique objects that have been buried by man. *Rikaz*, a general term encompassing *kanz*, refers to all valuable objects underground.

By broadly stating that "there is *humus* (one-fifth) on *rikaz*,"[16] the Noble Messenger (upon whom be peace) has obligated a *zakat* of one-fifth or, 20%, on all unearthed items. Taking this hadith as a starting point, the Hanafi school has decided that a 20% *zakat* must be acquired from all types of solid minerals that can be melted, like gold, silver, iron, copper and lead. No *zakat* is necessary, the school generally opines, from solid minerals unable to liquefy, such as rubies, emeralds, marble and lime, as well as liquid substances that are unable to naturally become solid, like crude oil and mercury. Although considering the generalized aim of the hadith, it would perhaps be more appropriate, especially today, to procure a 20% *zakat* from all types of *rikaz*. Besides, the transmitted hadith pertaining to the *zakat* of precious stones, technically, does not offer certitude. Thus it is more fitting to predicate the judgment on a proof of certainty, in addition to bearing in mind the principle of *maslaha* (common interest) and pay *zakat* regardless.

An emphasis on the customary aspect will be of further benefit. Insofar as commercial affairs are concerned, there is a great deal of difference between today and the early period of Islam. The demand toward precious stones then, surely, could not have been anywhere nearly as strong as it is today. For instance, petroleum, an item that has ultimately become an inseparable part of life and today's "black gold," was probably not even known back then; even if it was known, nobody could have predicted its countless potential uses. Hence, current supply and demand must be considered along with customs in determining what is and what is not subject to *zakat*.

In brief, taking the current situation into perspective, it is quite possible to appropriate 20% *zakat* on all types of excavated minerals. It has become somewhat impossible to exclude, from *zakat*, these precious minerals, especially petroleum, for which the mere acquisition results in such stormy global disputes.

CHAPTER 4

Who Is Obliged with *Zakat*?

WHO IS LIABLE FOR ZAKAT?

B efore collecting *zakat* from the obliged, it is essential to first ascertain who these individuals are. This requires certain prerequisites, like the knowledge of Islam, freedom, wealth, sanity, maturity—in addition to the requirements concerning wealth, namely ownership, augmentation, *nisab*, an elapse of a year and the exclusion of basic necessities.

Moreover, there are additional points pertaining to the collection of *zakat* that must crucially be observed. In sum, *zakat* must be requested strictly of those who are eligible, and eligibility demands certain requirements relating, in part, to the person in question, and in part, to the person's wealth.

WHAT FEATURES MUST ONE POSSESS
TO BE OBLIGED WITH *ZAKAT*?

These requirements can be encapsulated as follows: being a Muslim free of any constraints, possessing the ability to obtain basic needs, being free of debt, and having reached maturity, all of which demand a separate elucidation.

A. ISLAM

Before anyone, Islam addresses the believer, constructing its precepts on this solid foundation of belief. Therefore, as is the case with other responsibilities, the first requirement for *zakat* is being a Muslim. The requirement of those who have not accepted Islamic teachings but continue to live in Muslim lands is a simple tax, or *jizya*, identified by the government.

B. FREEDOM

Zakat has not been ordained compulsory on those enslaved or incarcerated; conversely, those in this situation are advised, firstly, to utilize their wealth, if they have any, to obtain their emancipation. From this perspective, slaves historically were not compelled with *zakat*, owing to their lack of physical freedom and their financial constraints.

C. BEING DEBT-FREE

Falling into debt, in normal circumstances, is something a Muslim should avoid, as it may involve entering the domain of subverting another's personal rights. The Prophet (upon whom be peace) had conceded to perform the funeral prayer of a deceased Companion only after another Companion agreed to finance his outstanding debts.[1] As the time and place of death of any one of us is unknown, the attitude of a wise Muslim would be to avoid, if possible, going into debt in the first place, as the hadith makes clear that dying while in debt can incur a difficulty for the community and a serious burden on our souls.

Critically, of course, Islam has never burdened man with obligations that exceed his capacity; contrarily, it has incessantly promulgated what is easy. This principle is also valid for *zakat*. Even though a person in debt may possess wealth which surpasses *nisab*, he is first advised to resolve his debts, and thus excused from *zakat*. People who find themselves in this position are, in fact, eligible to receive *zakat*, as testified by the Exalted Creator in the Qur'an.

D. SANITY-MATURITY

Maturity is the point where obligations start, and in effect, a child is not responsible until he or she reaches that phase. Perhaps some voluntary duties may be taken up for the sake of becoming accustomed to servanthood, although this does not imply an obligatory activity. The advice of the Noble Messenger, for example, is to accustom a child to *salat* (prayer) at the age of seven, and impart gentle words of encouragement if the child is still not offering *salat* at age ten. Yet again, the Messenger has pronounced that the *pen* (responsibility) has been lifted from a child until maturity, from a sleeper until he is awake, and from the insane until sane.[2]

WHAT ARE THE REQUIREMENTS OF THE PROPERTY SUBJECT TO *ZAKAT*?

Offering *zakat* necessitates the prior fulfillment of some requirements pertaining to wealth. Thus, as mentioned above, a person is obliged only to pay *zakat* on the possessions that meet these terms—namely, a person must possess the entire ownership of the wealth; the wealth must be augmentable; it must have surpassed the set amount well above the basic necessities; and a full year must elapse since its attainment. This description needs to be elaborated further at this point.

A. OWNERSHIP

In calling upon those obliged to perform their duties of *zakat*, Islam does not want them to pay *zakat* on the wealth they are yet to possess, a demand that would indubitably inflict people with financial hardship. Wealth is generally obtained by virtue of legitimate methods like earnings, inheritance, mutual agreements, donations, and so forth; hence, a person can freely dispose of and orchestrate his wealth, and take full responsibility in doing so. This, in turn, verifies the full ownership of wealth and therefore, within this framework, whichever method may be used in attaining this wealth, the owner meeting the requirements of full ownership must unavoidably pay its *zakat*.

1. Should zakat be given on loans?

In a case where a person is the creditor, that is, he possesses money that is temporarily lent to somebody else, we are faced with two outcomes in ascertaining the necessity of *zakat*.

Firstly, if the money that is expected to be paid back is under guarantee, like a check or promissory note seen as certain repayment, then this wealth is virtually commensurable with the wealth at hand, and as a result, its *zakat* must immediately be paid. Given that the chances of repayment are doubtful or improbable, then the *zakat* on this money should be delayed until reimbursement takes place. When the repayment does take place, we are then faced with another two alternatives: some scholars believe that as well as not giving *zakat* for previous years, the current year's should also be withheld, because in a sense, it resembles newly acquired wealth. The others, who approach the issue from the perspective of the rights of the poor, maintain that its *zakat* should still be offered. Insofar as caution is concerned, undoubtedly, the additional payment of the previous year's *zakat* is more appropriate, both as a means of steering clear from breaching the rights of the poor, as well as taking a step towards attaining the pleasure of God.

B. AUGMENTATION (THE INCREASE OF POSSESSIONS)

Islam does not necessitate *zakat* on property that by nature does not increase, though conversely, it targets augmentable possessions. Augmentation or *nama* denotes valuables that increase and attract revenue and earnings, and is classified into two: absolute augmentation and relative augmentation. Absolute augmentation is basically the increase of property or possessions through birth, reproduction, trade, or the like. Accordingly, animals or livestock, gold, silver and commercial merchandise fall under this category. Relative augmentation, on the other hand, is the wealth possessing possibility of increase at the hand of its owner or agent. Irrespective of whether the owner increases it or not, he will effectively be asked for *zakat* on that wealth, owing to its potential. However, in Islam, if the property is lost or stolen, and the owner consequently becomes power-less in its management, then he is not obliged with *zakat*.

C. NISAB (MINIMUM EXEMPTION LIMIT)

As mentioned earlier, *nisab* is the minimum extent which wealth must reach to become eligible for *zakat*. *Zakat* must imperatively be given of wealth that has realized that amount. As *zakat* is a critical means of social assistance, it would be meaningless and beyond its aim to either fail to implement such a measure or to demand everyone to pay from whatever trivial wealth they might possess.

Accordingly, the Prophet of Islam (upon whom be peace) has clearly identified the amount of *nisab* for each item. The *nisab* has been identified as 5 for camels, 30 for cattle, 40 for sheep, 85 grams for gold and 595 grams for silver. The *nisab* for commercial merchandise is established in concordance with gold and silver. As for agricultural harvest, the ratio is one-tenth for crops grown by rain-water or streams, or one-twentieth for crops grown through personal irrigation. For storable crops like wheat, barley and raisins, the *nisab* is 5 *wasq* (approximately 653 kg), and the prevalent conception is that no *zakat* is required for vegetables such as onions and lettuce. Abu Hanifa, however, maintains that regardless of their *nisab*, all agricultural goods, more or less, are subject to *zakat*.

Insofar as minerals and marine products are concerned, they do not possess a specific requirement for *nisab* and therefore their *zakat*, at any rate, must be paid. Because we have thoroughly handled the matter of *nisab* in the chapters concerning the recipients of *zakat*, those who desire more information are advised to throw a glimpse there.

D. THE WEALTH MUST EXCEED BASIC NECESSITIES

Another prerequisite for *zakat* is that the wealth should surpass the amount needed for sustenance, which may vary depending on social, economical and current circumstances. Nonetheless, there are always aspects on which all can mutually agree on, enumerated by the Hanafi scholars as consisting of basic food items, clothing, housing, enough wealth to see to one's debts, work utensils or apparatus, furniture, a means for travel—or, in today's conditions, a car or books needed for education. Moreover, the needs of those who, in Islam, are required to be taken care of—such as children, spouse, parents etc.— are similarly allowed basic necessities which are not liable to calculations of *zakat* upon the person providing their care.

E. THE ELAPSE OF ONE YEAR

For one to become obliged with *zakat*, at least a year has to elapse on the earnings beginning from the date of their attainment. This elapse of a year, called *hawalanu al-hawl* in Islamic terminology, is calculated in reference to the lunar year. However, this requirement does not necessarily aim at all types of wealth: it does pertain to livestock, money and commercial merchandise; but it does not affect agricultural crops, fruit, minerals, treasure, honey and similar items.

Another aspect needs to be elaborated. A person who continues to acquire new wealth in addition to the base wealth which has reached *nisab* and is thus subject to *zakat*, no longer needs to wait for the elapse of a year on these possessions; on the contrary, these augmentations need to be progressively included in the base wealth and calculated accordingly. This point is overwhelmingly agreed upon for commercial merchandise and for the offspring of livestock, although there is a minor difference of opinion between the schools pertaining to increases in different types of livestock. The general consensus, however, is that under such circumstances, one must start anew; for instance, if a person owns camels equivalent to *nisab*, for which he is paying *zakat*, and acquires a further 30 cattle or 40 sheep, he would wait a year for these new acquisitions, and then pay their *zakat*, owing to the difference of type. However, if the person is doing business with these animals, then without waiting for the elapse of a year, he must pay *zakat* on them. For this reason, if a person buys a further 100 sheep, for instance, in addition to the 40 sheep for which he is paying *zakat*, according to Abu Hanifa, he must provide *zakat* on 140 sheep without waiting for a year to elapse.

CHAPTER 5

How Is *Zakat* Paid?

Can *ZAKAT* be paid by way of estimation?

Islam permanently constructs its verdicts on robust foundations, thus guessing or estimating the amount of due *zakat*, a method prevalently resorted to in agriculture, is not desirable, simply because more often than not, the ultimate result does not match one's expectations. As a general tenet, the Messenger of God has forbidden agricultural trade based on assumptions, that is, before the ripening of crops. It is worth mentioning that the Messenger of God personally made assumptions on some crops before they matured and became manifest; scholars like Abu Hanifa and Sawri, however, contend that this was during a special circumstance concerning and exclusive to the Jews of Khaybar, and for that reason, it is not appropriate for us to conduct trade based on such assumption. Other scholars who permit estimation limit it strictly to grapes and dates, excluding all other types of produce. In view of the adopted course of action after the Prophetic Era, it may be said that although such conduct may be allowable for governments in order that they may attempt to balance the treasury from the perspective of income and expenses, adopting such a method for generally ascertaining *zakat* will inevitably result in uncertainty and/or error. Therefore, although estimation could be an approach espoused by some governments, it can, in no way, provide a consistent basis for an Islamic judgment pertaining to *zakat*.

Should *ZAKAT* be collected into the same fund?

Items collected as *zakat* must not be mixed with other taxes and revenues, as the Qur'an has specifically identified the targets of *zakat*. In addition, there are those who are ineligible to receive *zakat*.

Therefore, given that the collector is the government, *zakat* must essentially be collected and distributed in a different fund to avoid such a complication.

The following hadith transmitted by Anas ibn Malik is worth a highlight in terms of displaying the Prophet's scrupulous sensitivity concerning this issue: "One morning I took Abdullah ibn Talha to the Messenger of God only to see him with a tool in his hand, marking the *zakat* camels."[1]

As understood by the hadith, items that have arrived at the treasury as *zakat* are meticulously demarcated to avoid a possible muddle. This sort of sensitivity, as exemplified by the Prophet himself, is an incumbent duty on all who assume the responsibility for collection and distribution.

CAN *ZAKAT* BE PAID IN WORTH?

There is no harm in paying the amount of *zakat*, after it has been established, with a different type of value. In fact, this assertion can be found in the hadiths that identify the items subject to *zakat*. For instance, the fact a person can give a 4-year-old camel and sheep or its equivalent of 20 *dirhams*, instead of the one 5 year-old camel he was originally obliged with, upholds the general practice allowing such substitutions. Similarly, the Noble Messenger declared that the *zakat* on dates could be given with grapes, or vice-versa.[2]

Predicating its verdict upon the above and other proofs, the Hanafi school has accepted that *zakat* can be paid in worth, allowing the donor a choice. If desired, the *zakat* can be paid in kind; or, its worth can be disbursed in cash; or checks or bonds may be contributed—a practice widely used today.

IS *ZAKAT* PAID ON WEALTH UNDER SOMEBODY ELSE'S CONTROL?

Islam, as a basic principle, compels a person causing or instigating an action, whether it is good or bad, with some responsibilities. In a *hadith* encompassing broad meanings, the Prophet of Islam informed his followers that a person breaking new ground, good or evil, will share an equal reward or sin with those who follow in his footsteps. Another hadith, harmonious with this one, states: "A cause of an action is like its perpetrator."

It is renowned that a person who has his duty of *zakat* fulfilled by somebody else receives, through the cause, an invaluable opportunity of acquiring immense rewards, not to mention the rewards bestowed on the mediator. By informing about the great rewards awaiting the wife,[3] a slave,[4] and a guard[5] for mediating in such a beneficial practice, the Noble Messenger entirely encouraged this action. Though there are numerous hadiths in relation to this point, we will for the time being only contend with one: "There is equal reward for a husband whose wife, without squandering, gives from their food supplies; the same goes for a guard. They cannot deduct from each others benefits."[6]

WOULD INSULT AND SCORN ANNUL *ZAKAT*?

All wealth is God's alone and naturally, He can dispose of it as He wills. Thus, individuals "possess" wealth only to serve and only relative to the ultimate ownership of God. He gives unto and trials whom He wills, and withholds from and trials whom He wills. Thus, the wealthy paying *zakat* must entirely comprehend that what they possess has been bestowed unto them only temporarily and ultimately is not theirs. The real owner of the wealth is He Who has decreed *zakat*, Who additionally has identified its places of disbursement. Thus, at no point does a payer have the right to boast and brag about *zakat*, as he is only the agent of distribution, so to speak. A verse in relation to this states, *"O you who believe! Spend a part of what We have given you before that day arrives when there shall be neither trading, friendship nor intercession"* (Baqara 2:254). This clearly alerts and instructs humankind as to the ideal course of action.

Therefore a person, as a servant of God, in no way holds the privilege of embracing disdain for the intended recipients of *zakat*.

Furthermore, the Qur'an explicitly provides the following warning for those who are not able to infer such a conclusion from other Qur'anic passages:

> "O you who believe! Render not vain your almsgiving by taunts and injury, like those who spend their wealth only for ostentation, and believe neither in God nor in the Hereafter. Such men are like a rock covered with earth; a shower of rain falls upon it and leaves it hard and bare. They will gain nothing from their works. God does not guide the disbelievers." (Baqara 2:264)

From this perspective, *zakat* keeps the rich in line with *tawhid* (belief in the Oneness of God), while at the same time rescuing the poor from a financial oppression and effectively constructing a bridge that connects both sides of the community. Thus, today, we describe with pride how our predeseccors, having entirely grasped this notion, had a common practice of leaving pouches full of gold written on them in places easily accessible to the poor: "This is *halal* (permissible) for you to take." The objective was to prevent the poor feeling even a tiny bit of embarrassment or discomfiture.

IS IT BETTER TO GIVE *ZAKAT* SECRETLY OR OPENLY?

The comparative virtue of secretly and openly giving *zakat* or *sadaqa* differs according to place and time. Although it may be better, on occasions, to give openly, at other times, opting to pay secretly may provide a wiser option. Verses and hadiths elaborating on both these circumstances afford us different clues in relation to this point. For example, *"To give alms in public is good, but to give charity to the poor secretly is better for you and will atone for some of your sins,"* (Baqara 2:271) *"Those who spend their wealth by night and day, in private and public, shall be rewarded by their Lord"* (Baqara 2:274). Based on these Qur'anic statements, we ascertain the diverse benefits of secret and open charities depending on time and place. Yet, Muslim scholars have preponderantly advised an open payment of *zakat* while recommending the secret offering of other charities.

Though an open payment may act as an encouragement to others, a secret payment forestalls the emergence of vices, like pride, arrogance about one's means, and showing off. A person may be able to steer clear of these vices while performing *zakat*, which is, after all, an imperative obligation which is supposed to be performed with the intention of purifying the wealth; however, as for *sadaqa*, a voluntary activity, falling prey to these vices may come more easily. It is for this reason while enumerating the seven groups of people to be shaded under the shade of the Throne, on a horrendous Day where no other shade exists, the Messenger of God also includes, "those whose left sides are oblivious to what their right sides have given (as charity)."[7]

Therefore, it is essential to give voluntary *sadaqa* or charities secretly, and for this reason, it is said that a supererogatory *sadaqa* given in secret is 70 times more virtuous and valuable than that which is given openly. The Noble Messenger articulated the following: "Goodness never exhausts, sins are not forgotten, and God never dies; so do as you wish."[8] Indeed God is Alive and Eternal, a Watcher and Guard over all things perpetrated. As verified by this additional declaration: *"We have shown him the right path, whether he be grateful or ungrateful"* (Insan 76:3). In other words, human may either nurture a profound gratitude towards the Being Who has, through innumerable ways, made him aware of His transcendent existence, or ungratefully, throw into dissipation all his privileges, including himself, by shamefully choosing the path of disgraceful rebellion.

Note that giving explicitly may involve a degree of disdain on behalf of the benefactor as s/he acquires personal insight to the needs, condition, and circumstances of the beneficiary. In addition, a hadith such as, "The hand which gives is better than the hand which receives," might spuriously justify disdain in souls lacking full insight into the Message. But clearly, disdaining and abasing a Muslim has indubitably been decreed forbidden.

A further difficulty arises if the recipient is not known to be poor by the public—someone who has kept his/her need quiet, so to speak—in which case giving the *sadaqa* overtly may incur the ill-thought from both the donor and others that the recipient is accepting the donation without a genuine need. Here, then, is another example of how each act of faith becomes both an opportunity and a trial—for it is not right to indulge in such thoughts about others, and we risk rapidly and completely annulling any potential benefits to ourselves if we fail to check our tendencies to judge or criticize in this way. Thus, in order to fend of Satan's whispers and the personal embarrassment the poor may experience, the best method remains that of our predecessors—one in which we secretively place the *sadaqa* in a location which is easily accessible by those in need, and then swiftly leave.

Perhaps we could make an exception for those towering spiritual figures who, by virtue of having already conquered their own egos, are not easily affected by the side-effects which plague the majority, and by whose leadership in the field of charity, many more souls might be drawn into random giving. For these noble individuals, visibility in the act of *sadaqa* might be appropriate. But this would certainly be an atypical situation—not a recommended practice for the average person.

Putting the Qur'anic balance into the picture, it can be ascertained that, occasionally, it is preferable to opt for an open payment of *zakat*, however, as mentioned earlier: "*To give alms in public is good, but to give charity to the poor secretly is better for you, and will atone for some of your sins. God has knowledge of all that you do*" (Baqara 2:272). There is a balance, in other words. In similar fashion to *salat* (prayer) and *sawm* (fasting), the performance of obligatory actions is an instrument of public encouragement, as well as clearing its performer from likely incriminations. The highly potent and symbolic words of the Prophet in reference to those deliberately falling back from congregational *salats* were as follows: "I have contemplated leaving a deputy to lead, then burst in on those who, without excuse, fall back from *salats*, and set their houses ablaze." In addition, the outer manifestation of a life of faith, of an adherence to the practice of Islam, is not a trivial matter, as verified by another hadith "Whoever performs our *salat*, faces our *qibla* (the direction turned towards during *salat*, towards the Sacred Ka'ba), and eats what we slaughter is a Muslim under the guarantee of God and His Messenger."[9] In effect, the belief of a Muslim is reflected and generally understood by others in terms of the publicly performed obligatory deeds; therefore, there is benefit in offering these openly, to dispel any possible suspicion and spare witnesses from the easy temptation of judging another believer; in addition, public contributions of *zakat* provide an inspiration to those outside of the faith who might feel invited to submit after witnessing the all-encompassing mercy espoused by the Qur'an.

The actions of Abu Bakr and Ali, may God be pleased with them, who had totally comprehended the balance displayed in the Qur'an, are exemplary. The former, having had 40.000 *dirham*s worth of wealth, donated a quarter of it at night, another quarter at day, another quarter in secret and the last quarter in public; thus he actualized all the facets emphasized in the Qur'an. The latter openly donating his 4 *dirham*s, and then remarked, "O God, let this be an encouragement"; while during a secret donation, he prayed "Only for your sake my Lord." While giving at night, he prayed again: "May my night be alight;" and during the day, he uttered, "O God illuminate my day."[10] There it is: a display of the Companions' astounding sensitivity and their profound vitality in bringing Islam to life.

CAN DEFECTIVE PROPERTY BE GIVEN AS *ZAKAT*?

The awesome balance set by Islam in all fields is also visible in the fundamentals of offering and collecting *zakat*. While instructing the collectors to avoid collecting the "best possession," the benefactors are themselves encouraged to choose to give their *best* as an invaluable means of reaching the spiritual summit, a fact attested to by the Qur'an: *"You will not attain righteousness until you spend of what you love"* (Al Imran 3:92). Anas ibn Malik narrates the following in relation: "Of the *Ansar* (Medinan Muslims)," Abu Talha was one of the richest, and Bayruha—a garden across the *Masjid al-Nabawi* (the grand mosque at Medina), was his most beloved possession. The

Messenger of God, on occasions, used to enter it and drink from its clean water. When the verse, *"You will not attain righteousness until you spend of what you love"* (Baqara 3:92) was revealed, Abu Talha went to the Prophet and proclaimed the following: "If this is what the Almighty God has decreed in His Book, then from now on Bayruha, my most prized possession, is a charity for God. I anticipate its rewards and benefits from Him alone. O Messenger of God! Do with it as you wish." The Prophet responded delightfully, "How beautiful! This will bring a multitude of rewards and a copious recompense in the afterlife. I have heard your words on this subject, but if you ask me, divide it between your relatives," and upon this Abu Talha divided it between his relatives."[11] Indeed, it is evident that in order to become an ideal servant of God, one must donate, for His sake, one's most cherished items. Those who aspire to Paradise undoubtedly will present, with paramount pleasure, their best crops and produce.

In a hadith conveyed by Abu Hurayra, the Messenger of God reveals, "Whoever donates an amount equivalent to a handful of dates out of his pure earnings—and certainly God accepts only that is pure—God will take it and, just how one of you rears his foal, he will raise it to the size of a mountain."[12]

Through another hadith, again transmitted by Abu Hurayra, the Prophet earnestly announced, "O humankind! God is Pure and He only accepts what is pure. God has also commanded the believers what He has commanded the Prophets, namely *"O Messengers! Eat of the pure things and act with righteousness"* (Mu'minun 23:51); and for the believers, *"O you who believe! Eat of the good and clean things which We have provided for you, and be grateful to God, if it is He whom you worship"* (Baqara 2:172).

In tandem, a person must put himself in the shoes of the recipient, and thus avoid giving substandard or defective items. The Qur'an elaborates the following caution in relation to this very fact: *"...and seek not the bad (with intent) to spend of it (in charity)"* (Baqara 2:267). In other words, one must be absolutely alert in preventing any illicitness, such as this has been forbidden by God, from coalescing with one's donations—either accidentally or by virtue of neglect on our part.

Consequently, all manner of "filth" must be kept well at bay from honest and pure earnings, and the charity should be presented from the purest portion—the portion which the benefactor himself would gladly accept in the reverse scenario, were he to find himself the recipient instead. In practical terms, this means ensuring that gains are not secured through means which are, themselves, illicit; and to make certain that the offering meets the highest trade standard, in terms of both the quality of the goods and their real value.

During the blissful era of the Prophet, people used to leave bunches of dates at the *Masjid al-Nabawi* for the poor to eat. One day, after having seen a few defective bunches, the Prophet (upon whom be peace) pointed with his stick and said, "If the owner of this charity wished, he would have donated a finer bunch. Its owner will, in turn, be reciprocated with a similarly defective return in the afterlife."[13]

WHEN IS THE MOST VIRTUOUS TIME FOR OFFERING *ZAKAT*?

After having reached its *nisab*, a property on which a year has elapsed becomes subject to *zakat*. Yet, the generally prevalent practice is to offer it during the month of Ramadan. Although this remains the overall accepted routine, there are others who maintain that *zakat* should best be given before its deadline or during the season of harvest. All these views, certainly, are predicated upon various proofs, which can be recapitulated as follows.

A. PAYMENT DURING RAMADAN

The practice of giving *zakat* in Ramadan is by and large based on two notions—namely to benefit from the special month's blessings, and to put a smile on the faces of the poor in preparation for *Eid*. While it remains essential to perform deeds within their specific time frames and in line with their particular requirements, their performance at sacred times and places, it is hoped, brings even greater rewards. For instance, offering *salat* at the *Ka'ba* or *Masjid al-Nabawi* is considered more valuable in comparison to other places. This is actually implied by the words of the Noble Prophet, who declared that there are only three mosques in the world that, on their own, are worth traveling to—Ka'ba in Mecca, Masjid al-Nabawi in Medina, and Masjid al-Aqsa in Jerusalem.[14]

As for timing, the blessings of Ramadan are evidently manifest; it is considered the *"sultan"* of the other eleven months, containing a night superior to a thousand months. Therefore, completing an obligation like *zakat* within the parameters of Ramadan is believed to be an opportunity to greater rewards, as well as serving its prime role of relieving its benefactor from a compulsory duty in a timely, scheduled manner. Narrated by Anas ibn Malik, the ensuing hadith alludes to this. The Prophet was asked, "What is the most virtuous fast after the fast of Ramadan?" He responded, "The fast of (the months of) Shaban, in reverence to Ramadan." He was then asked: "Which *sadaqa* is of greater virtue?" And he replied, "*Sadaqa* given in Ramadan."[15]

B. PAYMENT BEFORE THE DEADLINE

The payment of *zakat* during Ramadan does not prevent it from being offered before this deadline. Also, there is no harm in offering *zakat* which is due between two Ramadans during the previous (first of these two) Ramadan. It is well renowned that Abbas, the uncle of the Prophet (upon whom be peace), had asked the Prophet whether it would be appropriate to give *zakat* before its due date, to which he has given an affirmative response, attested to by personal verification of the Prophet through the chain of Umar: "We received the due *zakat* of Abbas last year."[16] Thus, the gist of it all is that a person, without wasting time, must perform his obligations before the cut-off dates. All in all, there is no problem in paying *zakat* beforehand during the preceding Ramadan, for this is far preferable than being under the debt of *zakat*.

C. AVOIDING OVERDUE PAYMENTS

Irrespective of the circumstances, a person compelled with *zakat* by Islam should immediately fulfill this obligation. As for those with reasonable excuses, such as suffering financial strife, they have been excused in any case.

The Almighty has placed numerous cautions in His Book advising debtors to reimburse their debts without delay or otherwise face dire consequences. For instance,

> And spend of that which We have Provided you before death befalls any of you and he should say: "Reprieve me, my Lord, a while, that I may give charity and be among the righteous." (Munafiqun 63:10)

> Spend a part of what We have given you before that day arrives when there shall be neither trading, friendship or intercession. (Baqara 2:254)

In fact, the Qur'anic words, *"Pay the due thereof upon the harvest day,"* have been understood as a command by a considerable number of scholars, whereby palpable benefits derive from giving *zakat* promptly, as soon as crops and fruits are harvested.

On the other hand, a sudden and unexpected death may mean that a person will be commencing the afterlife in debt, as it is impossible for man to predict the place and time of his end. For that reason, it is crucial to constantly be aware of this reality. The Messenger of God refused to perform the funeral *salat* of a Companion until another Companion had agreed to pay his debt, as discussed earlier. This debt in question only pertained to personal rights, whereas the debt of unpaid *zakat* is even more serious in that it concerns both personal rights and the ultimate right of God; therefore, the latter burden is indisputably heavier. In emphasizing the importance of this responsibility, and in trying to thwart people from taking it on the lighter side, the Messenger of God instructed in the following way a Companion who wished to ascertain the most valuable charity: "It is the *sadaqa* you present while you are full of health, greedy towards riches, living with the fear of poverty, and desiring wealth. Don't you ever postpone this to your last breath, wherein you will say, 'This is his and that is hers.' But that would be worthless, as at any rate, your wealth has already become theirs!"[17] In a similar Qudsi hadith, the Almighty after illustrating the conceited nature of man, reprimands him: "You collect and then withhold, saying you will give at the moment of death. But isn't that a little too late?"[18]

WHAT ARE THE IMPLICATIONS OF DECEITFUL BEHAVIOR DURING PAYMENT OF *ZAKAT*?

No matter which action a person pursues, it will never escape the invincible, all-encompassing knowledge of God. In Qur'anic terms, though it may be the weight of a grain of mustard seed hidden in a rock or in the heavens or in the earth, in no way will it be beyond God's omniscience. Being the Creator of everything, He certainly knows all things committed by human, concealed or unconcealed. After gaining full comprehension of this reality, it is unthinkable for a believer to even attempt to transgress the limits and instructions regarding payment of *zakat*. For the others who are weak at heart, spellbound by the world's spurious luxuries, and who may resort to cheating their way out of *zakat*, the Messenger of God (upon whom be peace) addressed a simple but stern warning, as dictated to Abu Bakr and narrated by Anas ibn Malik: "Individual property cannot be separated in order to break free from the duty of *zakat*."[19]

For all intents and purposes, then, those fostering the anticipation that they might be able to break free from the duty of *zakat* are hopelessly trying to flee from an obligation decreed by God, simultaneously displaying a deceitful and swindling demeanor which is totally unacceptable for a Muslim to endorse. Irrespective of what the action may be, everything is being recorded, as we speak, to be exposed on a Day when all secrets will be revealed. Fleeing from such a duty, when a true Muslim should actually be searching for ways to donate more than the bare minimum, can only be explained by a weakness of *iman* (faith in God), and such a feeble *iman* is bound to cause grave impairments over time.

CAN PROPERTY GIVEN AS *ZAKAT* BE BOUGHT BACK?

Speaking in terms of trade, although there may be no problem in buying a charity item back, insofar as *zakat* is concerned, it is rather inappropriate. The most famous narration involving this scenario is that of Umar's, who had once given charity in the way of God, only to soon see it being up for sale at the market. Carrying the intention to repurchase that item, he went and asked the Prophet (upon whom be peace) whether it would be appropriate or not. The Prophet's response was, "Do not revert to your *sadaqa!*" In another version, the Prophet says, "Do not repurchase it, even if it could be sold to you for one dirhem, as reverting to *sadaqa* is like reverting to something you vomited."[20] Bearing in mind both the fundamental trade principles of Islam and the above hadith, the scholars have concluded that although such a trade is financially valid, it is ultimately attached to a large degree of inappropriateness and therefore discouraged. It is clear that, in this case, the verdict is influenced more by a socio-psychological incentive than a strictly jurisprudential one.

IS THERE A WORLDLY PUNISHMENT FOR UNSETTLED *ZAKAT*?

Being a financial obligation and a matter of concern for the entire community, *zakat* has necessitated the instalment of many incentives and deterring precautions against the evasion of payment—and appropriately so. Caliph Abu Bakr's explicit declaration to wage war against the deniers of *zakat*, and the scholars' agreement on the seizure of half the wealth of a withholder of *zakat*, can be considered as clear examples. As for the repercussions in the afterlife, we can only know what the Qur'an and Sunna permit, and due to our insufficiency in being able to entirely apprehend its nature, we leave the details with the Almighty and His Messenger. Simply put, acts of worship are constructed on faith, for which reason it is unthinkable for a true believer to abscond from duties pertaining to his/her servanthood. Nevertheless Islam, in allowing no vulnerabilities in the matter of *zakat*, and in preparing for weaknesses of faith, has prescribed certain laws to address the diverse attitudes exhibited by those whose own beliefs have not reached a level sufficient for appropriate self-monitoring on this important matter.

Eluding the duty of servanthood, Islam maintains, is all but equivalent to transgressing the borders of the religion itself. As *zakat* is an imperative social requirement incumbent on Muslim individuals, neglecting this worship cannot be passed over lightly, and Islam cannot remain indifferent to those who avoid *zakat*, and quite plausibly, will take firm precautions. To impose a fitting punishment, the scholars have agreed upon seizing half the property of a person resisting *zakat* out of avarice, as verified by the hadith conveyed by Muadh ibn Jabal, wherein the Messenger of God had announced, "Whoever gives *zakat* accepting a divine reward will receive just that; and whoever refuses, we will confiscate half his property as penalization. This is one of the definite verdicts of God. As for Muhammad's family, they have no share (i.e. they are ineligible to receive *zakat*)."[21]

WHAT IS THE PUNISHMENT FOR UNSETTLED *ZAKAT* IN THE HEREAFTER?

The mysteries of the Heavens, impossible for human to know, are only known to the Creator. The afterlife, as far as knowledge attained through human's endeavors is concerned, is also a mystery. God, however, Who is the Ultimate Knower of all mysteries, has provided us countless information concerning the afterlife, including the destiny of those who resist the payment of *zakat*. The following verses depict the ominous situations they are destined to face:

> Those who hoard up gold and silver and do not spend it in the way of God, give tidings unto them of a painful punishment. (Tawba 9:34)

> That which they hoard will be their collar on the Day of Resurrection. (Al Imran 3:180)

Moreover Sunna, the other half of revelation, contains additional reports in relation to this. The Messenger of God, as reported by Abu Hurayra and Jabir, said, "For those who deny the Right of God, as well as owning camels, cattle or sheep, their stock will return to them in the afterlife, more in numbers and larger than ever. The person will be seated in a straight and wide place wherein the animals, of which none have broken horns or are hornless, will begin to trample him. After the first round comes to an end, it will start again, and this process will continue until the verdict closes on all creatures. Again, if a person financially eligible for *zakat* refuses, then his wealth, in the Hereafter, will embody the appearance of snake, bold from excessive poison. The man will flee, only to find that each time the snake is relentlessly breathing down his neck; and it will be exclaimed to him, 'This is your wealth which you were so stingy over!' Finally, realizing there is no chance of escaping, the man will helplessly insert his hand into the snake's mouth, whereby the snake will commence torturing him by gnawing like a camel chewing crop."[22]

In another hadith, on the account of Abu Hurayra, the Prophet of Islam warned, "Gold and silver of which their rights (*zakat*) have not been presented will be brought on the Day of Judgment in the form of steel pillars, which will then be scorched and employed to brand their owners."[23]

CHAPTER 6

Where Is *Zakat* Given?

WHO ARE THE RECIPIENTS OF *ZAKAT*?

The Qur'an has explicitly delineated the recipients of *zakat* with the verse, *"Alms are only for the poor and the needy, and those who collect them and for those whose hearts are to be reconciled, and for the ransom of captives and debtors and for the way of God and for wayfarers"* (Tawba 9:60). In conjunction with the subtlety of the words encompassed by the verse, scholars have put forward various interpretations regarding whether *zakat* should only be given to those counted among the enumerated eight categories per se; whether they should all receive *zakat* equally; or whether it would be enough to donate the *zakat* only to one group. The uncertainty concerning the eligibility for *zakat* of some institutions carrying identical features of one or more among these eight groups has also been examined. At this point, it is important to put emphasis on each of these groups.

A. THE POOR

Right from the outset, scholars have found it difficult to place a clear-cut border between poverty and destitution. On occasion, the term "poor" denoted to those in need among the Muslim community, whereas "destitute" was the term given to the under-privileged among the non-Muslim minority. On still other occasions, regardless of the difference in faith, while the destitute signified the deprived who had divulged their needs to the public, the poor were needy who, out of self-respect, would not disclose their needs, as described by the Qur'an: *"...but you will know them by their appearance. They never beg of people with importunity"* (Baqara 2:273). Though they endure all kinds of financial difficulty without making themselves known, it is imperative that these, too, be identified and given *zakat* in order to become effectively liberated from their financial oppression—though such identification predicates some form of research.

As long as each of the eight categories possess these prerequisites, it is maintained, they will have the right to procure their share of *zakat*, just like shareholders do in a business enterprise. A person is continuously eligible to receive *zakat* provided that his degree of poverty remains unchanged, or at least remains below the poverty standard.

A few scholars, headed by the Shafii school, observe the situation from a rather unique perspective, insisting that the ultimate reason why the categories of poor and destitute have been mentioned separately, though they virtually hold the same meaning, is a result of the boundless compassion of God upon those in need, accentuating that when required, they are entitled to two-eights of an overall share of *zakat*. Thus the needy, by virtue of being named twice, in other words, can be eligible to twice as much *zakat* as others.

It is utterly impossible to obtain harmony in a society where one portion of people spend money like there is no tomorrow, and the other portion are left to sleep on the street. Expecting the impoverished, who are incessantly struggling with turmoil and hardship, to foster gratitude and sympathy for the rich, who are immersed in a life of luxury, amounts simply to being oblivious about natural human inclinations. However, it is important that one not exploit the issue of poverty by despoiling the wealth that instigates another, different imbalance—like some dubious systems have done in recent history. As it does in all other aspects, Islam strictly recommends a balanced approach in this issue also. In the very beginning of the chapter of *Rahman*, a declaration of Divine Compassion, the Qur'an accentuates the importance of moderation and a balanced life, stressing that harmony between individuals can only be upheld through embracing the equilibrium between rich and all kinds of *zakat* recipients.

B. The destitute

The destitute are the second group assigned by the Qu'ran to receive *zakat*. According to the majority of scholars, the term "*miskin*" or destitute denotes someone who, out of helplessness, takes care of his necessities openly through the publication of his need. Most of the time, such pitiful plights become manifest, simply from their deplorable living standards and their depleted states, inevitably making it amply evident to the public that they live in very disadvantaged circumstances. The Qur'an describes a destitute person as, *"...a poor wretch in misery,"* (Balad 90:16) illustrating the multi-dimensional aspect of their anguish.

Contrary to the prevalent meaning assigned to the term, according to the Noble Prophet, a *miskin* (destitute person) is not a person who walks around begging for money; more exactly, a destitute is one who while he is in need, his need is not taken note of and for this reason, he doesn't receive any share of charity. By synoptically looking at the general structure of hadiths, we find that what the Prophet did was to correct a term wrongly used in society, an action corroborated by the Qur'an *"...they never beg of people with importunity"* (Baqara 2:273). During one instance, in fact, in returning proper meaning to the term, the Noble Messenger explained: "A destitute person is not a beggar who is banished with a couple of dates or one or two morsels. A destitute person is a model of dignity and purity." And in the Qur'an, we find the purest form of corroboration: *"They never obdurately beseech of people."*[1]

The late professor Muhammad Hamidullah made a rather original commentary on the issue, which was alluded to in a general fashion above. Destitute persons, according to Hamidullah, are those in need from among the Jewish and Christian minorities, a view that if accepted, would explain the policy promulgated by Caliph Umar in providing regular payment for the non-Muslim minorities. At any rate, this view is interesting to consider.

C. ZAKAT COLLECTORS

As it is understood both from the expressions used in the verse and the practice of the Prophet in this area, the organization regarding collecting and administering *zakat* should be managed from a single center. Even though an individual can fulfill his duty by person-ally locating and disbursing his own *zakat*, it must be remembered that Islam, at the same time, is religion of orderliness with a high-ly developed regard for community; therefore, it has not left on its own a duty that is a potential conciliator between members of a society.

The first application that comes to mind at this point is when the Prophet sent Muadh ibn Jabal to Yemen as a *zakat* collector, in addition to assigning him several other duties.[2] Second, he also dis-patched Ibn Lutaybiyya to the tribe of Bani Sulaym as a *zakat* col-lector, and concomitantly demanded a report upon Ibn Lutaybiyya's return.[3] As a third reference, the Prophet delivered a sermon to the Companions on behalf of a collector who had arrived with, as he called it, "additional gifts." All of these instances corroborate the general understanding that during the time of the Prophet, *zakat* was collected from a single center.

Warning the official collectors against oppression and justice, the Prophet also issued a reminder to the public, advising them to be kind towards the collectors. Instructing Muadh to "take their *zakat* but avoid seizing their best possessions,"[4] the Messenger had also recommended the public that they, "Send away the collectors in high spirits."[5] On the whole, the Messenger of God, in address-ing those obligated with *zakat*, stated, "When a *zakat* collector comes to you, makes sure he leaves contented."[6] The idea, of course, was to encourage donors to understand the positive spirit in which giving should take place, in consideration of its high ben-efit for both themselves and the community. Yet again, we are wit-ness to the brilliant balance established by Islam in all arenas.

So basically, a *zakat* collector is a person who officially, on behalf of the Government, devotes his time and effort towards the duty of collecting *zakat*. Therefore, and quite plausibly so, he needs a certain salary to make ends meet. In the precious words of the Prophet, "Till his return home, a *zakat* collector is like a *ghazi* (warrior), bat-tling in the way of God."[7] Authorizing a warrior's share of booty after battle, Islam thus necessitates a certain share for the collector, to be extracted from the gathered *zakat*. In fact, the Messenger of God denied the request to refuse payment, such as was made by the likes of Umar, rejoining: "Take it. If you have no need for it, then give it to somebody else." Based on this, Umar, during his days as caliph, methodically allocated a certain share to all *zakat* collectors, irrespective of their wealth, and regardless of their requests to refuse such payments.

Based on the above principle, some have maintained that a certain share of *zakat* should be allocated for all government employees. In the case of a government which is very successful in fairly collecting *zakat* by virtue of the better organization of its collectors, revenue will begin to infiltrate from all corners, and this will result in greater numbers of needy people receiving the benefits of such collections—from wheat, to barley, to all sorts of agricultural harvests, and barring the view of Abu Hanifa, including vegetables and fruits, also. Moreover, the collector, full of goodwill, will visit all enterprises, from crude-oil wells to mine shafts; he will oversee all hordes of grazing sheep and cattle; and he will diligently inspect every single item of wealth and treasure to make certain that not a single hungry mouth is deprived of his or her rights. Such altruistic officials, sacrificing their time and efforts for the good of the community, should obviously not be abandoned to beseech others for their own sustenance and, thus, must be allocated a payment from the collected *zakat*. Irrespective of the personal wealth of collectors, then, it is imperative that the Qur'an and Sunna are abided by and the all those who engage in this noble act are given *zakat*. This issue holds another dimension, too. Taking care of the needs and salaries of those employed in duties involving such large stakes will effectively discourage corruption, in addition to enhancing "employee motivation." The espousal of this attitude by our predecessors is highly admirable, especially that of the Ottoman State, which owed its prolonged existence to its meticulous and judicious management of *zakat* collection. The allotment of *zakat* to collectors effectively prevented them from condescending to bribery or other possible enticements, thus sturdily barring probable loopholes. The alternative outcome would almost certainly be insurmountably and perva-sive corruption. Such is Islam and the precepts it propounds. It con-siders, on the one hand, the needs of the collector and by taking care of each such individual, elevates the collector from personal abase-ment; on the other hand, it instills in each collector the importance of living a just and prudent life in preparation for the Day of Judgment, rendering in practical terms the most critical aspects of Islam.

D. *MUALLAFA AL-QULUB* (THOSE WHOSE HEARTS ARE TO BE RECONCILED WITH ISLAM)

Another group deserving *zakat* are those whose hearts are on the grip of reconciliation with Islam. Depending on the intention of the various approaches, this group can be classified as follows:

a) Those who, although Muslim, do not yet have faith entrenched in their hearts.

b) Those non-Muslims whose hearts are attempted to be rec-onciled with Islam.

c) Those non-Muslims who harbour hostilities towards Islam, but whose aggression or resentment may be preventable.

The Prophet (upon whom be peace) indeed allotted *zakat* for all of the people in the above categories. As for the likes of Abu Sufyan, who had become Muslim but was yet to develop maturity in his belief, the Messenger ultimately won his heart—and count-less others—by virtue of granting *zakat* copiously, a practice of gen-erosity which effectively established a positive belief in the hearts of the recipients. Abu Sufyan, once he became a Muslim, fervently desired to join his son, Iqrimah, at the fierce Battle of Yarmuk during the time of Caliph Umar—his courageous aspirations affirming a deeply ensconced faith whose seeds were initially sewn with the gift of such benevolence.

When the Messenger of God gave 100 sheep to Safwan ibn Umayya, he accepted Islam with an ardor worth the expense of perhaps 10,000 sheep, and this offering simultaneously hastened his realization of a great and precious degree of faith, as verified by his subsequent words; "Out of all men, the Prophet was the one I was most infuriated with. On the day of Hunayn, however, he gave so much that he suddenly became my most beloved."[8] The recipients were so much touched by the kindness and generosity of the Prophet and came to the understanding that he was divinely led. They soon joined him and their lasting faith soon made them exemplary figures in the service of God. Another group consisted of some Bedouins who had given in to Islam, although a pure *iman* (faith) had not yet sunk into their hearts. To state it more explicitly in Qur'anic terms, they were saying, "we believe," although they had only surrendered: *The Bedouins say "We believe." Say: "You do not; rather say 'we profess Islam,' for faith has not yet entered your hearts"* (Hujurat 49:14).

This reference clearly accentuates the fact that *iman*, belief in God, is a divine gift, attained only through man's investigation, identification and application of his belief in the inextinguishable Celestial Flame. As far as the Bedouins were concerned, they had only resigned themselves to the splendor of Islam, as their hearts were not mature enough then to fully come to grips with faith. Thus the Messenger of God was prudently allocating a share of *zakat* for them, in hope of decreasing their distance to the ideal faith. When Safwan ibn Umayya was given 100 sheep and 100 camels, for instance, he exclaimed to those around him, "By God! Hasten to submit to this man, for he has no fear of his wealth running out,"[9] acknowledging the Prophet's dependence on God, Whose treasures never cease. By receiving *zakat*, those on the border between belief and non-belief swiftly had their pendulum swung towards the most excellent direction, commencing to quench their hearts with the satiating fountain of faith.

Yet another group were the vanguards of polytheists reputed with sordid behaviors. Through offering these people *zakat*, the Messenger of God was effectively repelling their potential for harming the community, as well as laying the groundwork for their future acceptance of Islam. This is exemplified by the saying, "Do good to whom you fear evil from." It is an important strategy to predict probable harm and deflect it with good, as man is inherently a servant of goodness. Such an approach, time and again, disperses possible damage and destruction before it even begins to form and creates a fresh breathing space for Muslims, whereby accumulated wealth is utilized to convert evil into good, as man earnestly acts upon the obligations of his servanthood to God.

In the words of the Qur'an, *"Vile women are for vile men, and vile men are for vile women"* (Nur 24:26). Evidently, by virtue of integrating these *muallafa al-qulub* into the picture, the Messenger of God instigated a series of multi-faceted benefits. Through receiving *zakat*, these people providentially gained profoundness in their faith; those oscillating between belief and unbelief opted for the former; and the leaders among the unbelievers, influenced by the generous grant, laid down their guns, providing amnesty for Muslims living under their control. The issue additionally has a financial component. Although the Prophet granted wealth to the leaders of the community, this act of giving entailed returns of abundant proportions. Because they enjoyed the benefits of receiving *zakat*, unbelievers granted certain essential permissions and rights to the Muslims under their control, who were then better able to offer *zakat* themselves; thus, the relatively trivial amount given to the leaders afforded large populations of Muslims the means by which they could honor their obligation to give *zakat* flowing into the pockets of the destitute. By this means, Muslims still managed to guarantee the general welfare of any community of which they were a part. In addition, the practice proved to be advantageous for the Muslims in more ways: it gave them the opportunity of fulfilling their obligations as well as bestowing on them relative freedom and autonomy, in addition to enshrining basic values of righteousness in the name of Islam in whatever community, and whatever time, Muslims happened to be.

This situation lasted until the period of Caliph Abu Bakr. One day, certain people who used to receive a share of *zakat* at the time of the Prophet came to the Caliph asking for money. The Caliph consented to signing their document of eligibility, which they took to

Umar, who was in charge of the treasury on that day. Who knows—perhaps Abu Bakr, an exemplary character filled with astounding mildness and compassion, simply wished to solve the matter without causing even the scantiest dissension within the caliphate. So he deferred the matter to Umar.

After receiving the document, Umar's sharp gaze oscillated between the document and those who had brought it. Though it is impossible to illustrate exactly what went through his mind in that instant, looking at the ensuing events, it seems most likely that Umar ascertained that Islam had now fully realized its splendor and unbelief had been dashed against the rocks. In effect, Islam, increasingly consolidating its eternal impressions on the world, was now standing on its own two feet.

As Umar also knew very well, *zakat* depended on specific circumstances, namely the existence of a given situation and people who fit the criteria of "need" under such circumstances. Umar, evidently and rightly content that the Arabian Peninsula was now the strong domain of Islam, tore the document and responded to the letter-holders by saying, "This is unacceptable. Go and work! In the days when you were given *zakat*, Islam was not standing on its own feet; but now, it is majestic and has no need of you!" As the Muslim community was firmly established, such a group of potential tormentors failed to meet the definition of a group whose hostilities to be prevented. Thus, it was no longer a necessity to pay *zakat* to those holding a sort of position of power.

Facing an unexpected situation, they promptly went to the Caliph, protesting, "Who is the Caliph, you or him? You sign the document and he tears it!" Abu Bakr simply replied, "If he liked, he would have been the Caliph," delivering a deeply meaningful and concise response to a group who had made a habit of freeloading.

Consequentially, the practice of giving *zakat* to the *muallafa al-qulub*, ended by the matchless vision and intelligence of Umar, has since provided material for diverse interpretations. The truth is, the Companions, gathered soon after the event, reaching a consensus that a share no longer needed to be allotted to those whose hearts are attempted to be reconciled with Islam, owing to the simple fact that the need no longer existed. However, this was the reflection of the social structure in relation to that particular verdict, as the need to appease others in this way had apparently ceased.

Some have interpreted the above event as an abrogation or *naskh* of a verse by the *ijma* (consensus) of the Companions, which can only be labeled as a blatant misunderstanding. Although the abrogation of one verse by another, or a sunna act by another, is acceptable, the abrogation of a sunna act by a Qur'anic verse, or even vice-versa, has been an issue of dispute, where most scholars have maintained implausibility of either. Thus, even the Prophet's words have no authority over the Qur'an, and it is thus utterly unthinkable for the Companions' consensus to presume or exercise a similar authority. As a result, the Qur'an cannot be abrogated by methods of deduction such as *ijma* (consensus) or *qiyas* (analogy).

Debates as such reveal a lack of understanding of the intent of this decision. When arriving at their verdict, none of the Companions— including Abu Bakr or Umar—carried even the slightest desire to abrogate the Qur'an; rather, their verdict was simply an end shot of sincere and proper brainstorming, a discussion, such of which is strongly encouraged in Islam. It is worthy to note that among the eight groups of recipients, the *muallafa al-qulub* have no particular prerequisites; hence, whatever is applicable to them is also applicable for the other groups. In a society where the poor and the destitute cease to exist, for instance, the need to give these two groups *zakat* concomitantly ceases, as was the case during the era of Umar ibn Abdulaziz. During that time, nobody dared to claim, "Umar ibn Abdulaziz abrogated the Qur'an," precisely because the events were unfolding exactly in concordance with the Prophet's (upon whom be peace) glad tidings of many years before.

So, too, the issue of *muallafa al-qulub*, had unfolded along a natural course. As is the case today, however, many refer to Umar's mentioned application when discussing those individuals and groups in various societies today who may nurture the intention of antagonizing the precepts of Islam. In fact, the new outcrop of such antagonists is entirely analogous to how the poor—who became increasingly hard to find during the caliphate of Umar ibn Abdulaziz — reemerged after the time of Umar ibn Abdulaziz. There were increases in debtors and even stranded traveler for that matter, individuals who only receive *zakat* provided that they exist. Therefore, those who claim that Umar abrogated a verse actually lack an adequate insight into the issue. Looking from the perspective of the Qur'an, the duty of *zakat* is not attached to certain individuals; rather, it is attached to certain needs, in so far as these reflected weaknesses of heart. Once these needs are taken care of, then these needs obviously no longer exist. Logically put: the attachment of the verdict to a certain cause necessitates the existence of that cause for its validity; therefore, the solution is pre-empted if the cause disappears, and then simply comes back into effect upon the future re-emergence of the need. Umar's verdict was clearly an appropriate jurisprudential response to the changing times and a further reflection of the comprehensive and vibrant nature of the Qur'anic message, which remains vital and eminently applicable under the most extensive variations in both temporal and physical circumstances.

The reason for the extended discussion of this issue is to emphasize the necessity of reviving this practice as a contingency given the current need which is arising in societies around the globe, and most particularly in the secular west. In this day and age, in fact, we suddenly find ourselves readily able to identify a great many people who can easily fit into the category of *muallafa al-qulub*. If we can successfully revive the practice of giving generously of *zakat* to mollify potential aggressors and avoid potential hostilities, then we may perhaps appease volatile characters, effectively providing them the priceless opportunity to gain acquaintance with Islam—and thus allow Muslims all over the world greater freedom and safety to express the full dimensions of their faith. Moreover, by exercising an important point of jurisprudence in recognizing the existence of *muallafa al-qulub* in the present day, our aim to spread the Islamic message to the four corners of the world, to invite to Islam as we are strongly ordained to do, will be facilitated by the effective removal of possible impediments, personal or governmental, that stand in our way. This is an excellent opportunity, in fact, for so-called "modern man" to accomplish superb feats to inject the Islamic spirit into thirsty hearts. The view of Imam Qurtubi, a scholar of the Maliki school, concords: "At other times, those who are bordered by non-believers should also offer this fund lest they transgress the border," This critical idea certainly deserves a special emphasis as the optimal framework for a contemporary approach to the full and peaceful existence of practicing Muslims in predominantly non-Muslim regions of the world.

As for today, there are many distinguished people, in educational, political, or socio-cultural arenas, who daily face the invitation to become the mouthpiece of others. The proper application of *zakat* under such circumstances, in line with the argument presented above, would ensure that their invaluable energies and capabilities do not become channeled towards causes devoid of scruples and deterring from righteousness, oppressing those who choose to practice their faith, both privately and publicly. For tragically, while these individuals generally set out to serve humanity and uphold virtue, they all-too-often become mere representatives of detrimental factions.

This approach would simply be an expression of familiarity with the true intent of the consensus of the great Companions on this subject, as well as with the Qur'an. For resuscitating the practice of giving *zakat* to the *muallafa al-qulub* would only lead us in the footsteps of Umar, who demonstrated so unequivocally the vibrant and effective nature of Islamic jurisprudence.

E. SLAVES

Slaves constitute one of the eight possible groups of recipients. As a basic principle, Islam is against the notion of slavery, desiring human to be liberated from all kinds of restraints through an assertion that their servanthood is only to God. The principles Islam has put forth have constantly paved the way for freedom, a value confirmed by many hadith concerning slaves, as the following exemplifies: "Feed them what you feed yourselves, clothe them what you clothe yourselves, do not impose on them duties they cannot bear, and treat them humanely."[10]

The world, however, has never been home only to Muslims. At various stages of history, wars have been waged against those attempting to extinguish the light of Islam, and as an upshot and a primarily reciprocal procedure, there were many captives taken. This was really the prevalent practice of the warfare of the period, one equally upheld and perpetrated by all sides. Suddenly eliminating slavery on a global scale would involve innumerable intricacies and countless reforms; the best thing to do, insofar as Islam was concerned, was to treat captives with utmost kindness and consideration, in order to use the times of captivity as an opportunity not to exploit other human beings, but to warm hearts towards Islam.

Accordingly, and due to many benefits, a certain share of *zakat* was allocated to slaves and those in captivity. It will be of further benefit to lay special emphasis on the fact that slavery is not an institution inaugurated by Islam; in addition, from a global historical perspective, the birth of Islam coincided with a period wherein humans were sold as slaves and even free men were under the constant threat of enslavement as a result of sudden raids. Islam, always and ever a religion of pragmatic, applicable, and comprehensive solutions, resorted to combating this problem gradually, imposing at every chance the very principles which would bestow first inner, then outer, freedom to slaves. This is certainly in keeping with one of the most basic tenets of Islam, which is that everyone is as equal as the spikes on a comb and the only superiority which should be sought is in terms of piety.[11] Here, then, are some of the key principles relating to slavery:

- The emancipation of slaves in return for some work or their value (*muqataba*),
- Emancipation by giving birth to the owner's child (*ummu walad*),

– Emancipating a slave to compensate for an unobserved vow,
– Emancipating a slave as compensation for *zihar* (the forbidden practice whereby a husband draws a resemblance between his wife and his mother as a pretext for divorce),
– Emancipating a slave as compensation for unintentionally causing death.

Visibly and unequivocally, Islam opened the doors to freedom wide open, constantly reiterating the multitudes of rewards entailed by the act of emancipating a slave, an act incessantly encouraged by God. Today, slavery in its full sense of the term does not exist although this is not to say that it will never come back into existence. Similar to the cause of *muallafa al-qulub*, and applying the same standard of jurisprudence, the reemergence of slavery would automatically resuscitate the practice of offering them *zakat*. Perhaps in this day and age, the issue may have switched to another level, or another forum. Even though physical slavery may have become obsolete, many people now have their feelings, thoughts and intellects enslaved, and thus are in dire need of genuine emancipation. Providing them some *zakat* would presumably be a means of dispersing from their minds these ill thoughts, beneficially opening their mind to the reality of a relationship with their Creator.

F. Debtors

In normal circumstances, *zakat* should be given to a person in debt, irrespective of the person's prior wealth. Although in one way, debtors can actually be classified among the poor and destitute, the main difference is that their unfortunate state is presumably only temporary. By declaring, "Charity is not permissible for the rich, except for the following five: A warrior in the way of God, a *zakat* collector, a debtor, a person who buys the charity collected as *zakat*, and a rich person who receives from a poor the gift that was given to him as *zakat*,"[12] the Prophet has pronounced the eligibility for *zakat* of a debtor, even if he is rich. On the account of Abu Said al-Hudri, a Companion during the time of the Noble Messenger had bought fruit, which were destroyed before he could offer their payment. Upon hearing this, the Prophet advised the others to lend him financial support. After the amassed total fell short of the required amount, the Prophet said to the creditors, "Take from what there is, for there is no more," insisting on some additional understanding and compromise on their behalf.[13] Falling into debt must never be seen as a method of receiving *zakat* or as a pretext for escaping it, practices strongly condemned by the Prophet and certainly subject to divine fury. The people declared by Islam as being eligible for *zakat*, in this case, are not those who are penalized for their avarice, but rather those who are going through rough patches while leading a planned and moderate life. The bottom line is that life is transient, man is expected to behave responsibly, and errors perpetrated in this fleeting life may lead to a devastating scenario on the Day of Judgment.

G. *FI SABILILLAH* (IN GOD'S WAY)

In line with the various connotations the Arabic term may suggest, *"fi sabilillah"* is basically the commitment to put aside all personal duties and dedicate one's entire time to spend in the way of God. Initially, this involves seeking and learning the knowledge that brings happiness in this life and in the hereafter, and in time, may also require the removal of impediments that stand in the way of spreading God's name to all corners of the world. It is exactly for this reason that a group courageously taking such an immense task is entitled to *zakat*, thereby encompassing the broader meaning of the term *jihad,* as all kinds of struggle offered with the sole aim of pleasing God.

Analyzing the issue from the perspective of the Prophetic Era, the *Ashab al-Suffa* (Companions that had dedicated their entire time to the pursuit of knowledge), whose numbers reached up to 400, throw more light on the issue as exemplary models, in terms of the duty they had accomplished. Enduring a variety of difficulties, they nevertheless remained incessantly alongside the Prophet, eager to realize his very command and imbibe from him pearls of wisdom. Having devoted themselves solely in this direction, they frequently suffered hunger, even facing, on occasions, the threat of falling unconscious. Abu Hurayra, an heroic example of this devotion, responded to certain criticisms that came in his direction by simply stating, "My brothers complain that I narrate too many hadiths. However, while my *Ansar* brothers (Medinan Muslims) were busy cultivating their lands, and my *Muhajir* brothers (Meccan Muslims) were engaged in trade, me and others alike were incessantly by the side of the Prophet, memorizing his words, "At the risk of fainting from hunger."[14] This illustrates the extent of the dedication and consequent hardship which devout followers encountered for the sake of serving the Qur'an and the Sunna—and also exemplifies the different manner in which believers struggled to support Islam. Of course, the Qur'an is far from quiet on such sacrifices, eternalizing their earnest devotions as follows, in a verse which was also critical to some of the earlier discussions:

> Alms are for the poor who are restrained in the cause of God, unable to travel in the land. The ignorant man counts them among the wealthy because of their restraint. But you will know them by their appearance. They never beg people with importunity. And whatever good things you spend, surely God knows them well. (Baqara 2:273)

Despite of the difficulties they constantly faced, these Companions would not divulge their hardships, causing others to overlook them when they identified people in no need. Even though there still were a limited number of individuals who might have had a fairly good idea of their dire situation, it was impossible to know the full depth of suffering they concealed to establish the faith of Islam. To cut a long story short, the following account provides an excellent example by which to crystallize this description.

Said ibn Musayyab, one of the forerunners of the *Tabiun* generation (the praised generation who were acquainted with the Companions, though they did not see the Noble Prophet himself) who was the son-in-law of Abu Hurayra, tells the following story about his father-in-law, as the elder walking around gleefully in a linen robe:

> Plunged in deep thought, he (Abu Hurayra) then turned to himself, muttering "Get over yourself, Abu Hurayra! You seem to have long forgotten the days when you would collapse from hunger and children would start treading on you, and others would hasten to you, conceiving it as an epileptic fit. Nobody would understand, bar the Prophet (upon whom be peace) and Jafar ibn Abi Talib, who would say 'Come Abu Hurayra!' whereupon you would tag along with them. How many times you entered the home of the Honorable Prophet, satisfying your hunger with milk, presented by him!"[15]

Abu Hurayra, in fact, could not pursue anything else, conceiving this as the only path to revive one's world and reach the eternal abode. Abu Hurayra's desire and sensitivity in running to the need of the Prophet, and in memorizing every single word he uttered, was equally matched by his vigor in joining the armed forces, when required, where he confidently assumed the front ranks. Similarly, Abu Lubaba, and many others, displayed the same attitude.

Thus it was for the likes of these exemplary figures, that divine glorification was revealed. As conveyed, there were more than 100 Companions who, while prostrating in *salat* (prayer), would hold fast to their insufficient clothes to prevent an exposure of their private areas. As a matter of fact, all possessions and wealth had been abandoned in migrating from Mecca to Medina for the sake of God. The Prophet (upon whom be peace) nurtured a unique sensitivity for his Companions, and he would give them everything that came his way; and yet, especially in the early years of the faith, it still fell short of covering even their basic needs. He himself would endure days of starvation, to the point where he even tied a rock around his stomach to diminish his own feeling of hunger—and yet his soft heart could not bear the hunger of his Companions. So while he lived a life well below the standards of those around him, he displayed an unmatched sensitivity to the requirements of others.

Through his efforts, Abu Hurayra achieved such proximity to the Messenger that more often than not, he would refer to the Prophet as his *Khalil* (Confidant), such that he would begin his explanations by saying, "My Confidant told me..." Or, "I went next to my Confidant." Or, "I conversed with my Confidant..." and so on. By using this term, Abu Hurayra alluded to the ache and longing he experienced whenever he was away from the presence of the Prophet. In one of his many visits to the Prophet, he witnessed him offering *salat* while seated, showing signs of agony and distress. Immediately after the *salat* was finished, Abu Hurayra asked the Prophet why he offered his prayer sitting, only to receive this response: "Hunger; O Abu Hurayra!" Abu Hurayra, having witnessed such a heartbreaking scene, broke down in tears and the duty of consolation was, again, left to the Prophet, who uttered these words of gentle comfort: "Don't cry, Abu Hurayra, because surely, the least torment on the Day of Judgment will befall the starved who have indeed already suffered its hardships."[16]

Such was the attitude displayed by this great "Confidant." While the Prophet endured a variety of hardships, it would obviously have been utterly unconceivable for Abu Hurayra and the other 400 friends – the *Ashab al-Suffa* – to opt for lives of pompous luxury. Affirming their faith in God granted them such an immense maturity that they were constantly on the lookout for opportunities where they could lend their services. So even while they lacked the basic necessities of the day—a horse to ride, a saddle, a flask to carry water in, or a loaf of bread, for example—they would still come to the Prophet, asking for opportunities by which they could serve in God's cause and thus vehemently insisting, "Provide us with means, O Messenger!" Evidently, the Companions always sought additional opportunities by which they could support the growth of their faith community and offer themselves increasingly in the name of God. Of course, understanding the depth of service of his close Companions, the Honorable Prophet would give them support and suggestions, as well as anything material he could provide, in order to increase their benefits before God. On the sad occasions when he had nothing left to give, and he was starving himself, he would suffer the unparalled and additional agony of having to turn back a Muslim who was willing to do more for his faith but simply had nothing more to offer. The Qur'an's depiction of the preparations in the lead-up to the Tabuk campaign draws attention to this profound and moving situation:

> Nor (is there any blame) on those who came to you, to be provided with mounts, and when you said to them, "I am unable to provide you with mounts." They returned with tears streaming from their eyes, grieving that they could find no means to contribute. (Tawba 9:92)

As mentioned earlier, it is unimaginable in any healthy community for the rich to indulge in luxury while there are those who, out of insufficient means, are deserted to their own starvation and despair. Therefore, mobilizing all financial means towards those who have dedicated their entire lives for a noble cause—and who shed tears not for their own discomfort, but only for their failures in finding the necessary means to give more—would ultimately revive their vanished hopes, instigating an immensely efficacious movement by which the rewards of overwhelming sacrifice would be jointly shared—and enjoyed—by all the benefactors. Within the broadest sense of the term, the invaluable groundwork would thus be laid for talented students and followers, germinating in them an enormous eagerness to become passionate servants in God's way, and upholders of universal ethics. This is, after all, the essence and vision of Islam.

H. WAYFARERS

On the word of the Qur'an, the last group of recipients which is identified is that of wayfarers—individuals who become needy during travel, even if they are essentially rich back home. It has virtually become impossible, especially today, to avoid traveling, whether it be for work or to spread the word of Islam to all the ends of the world. The quest to travel in order to serve in God's way; to provide a righteous example of faith in parts of the world with little or no exposure to Islam; or to resettle in different communities in order to directly invite others to Islam is, in effect, an excellent motive to establish funds, in concordance with the Qur'anic directive to accommodate the needs of travelers and those who lend their services to the mission of God.

This command is simultaneously a verification of how Islam attends to a person's financial requirements while also decreeing the spread of good and the purge of evil—for including these altruistic souls as recipients of *zakat* allays their financial concerns and saves them from lagging behind in devoting their lives to the search for thirsty hearts eager to be quenched with the nectar of Truth.

The Messenger of God enunciated the rich among those who may occasionally be eligible to receive *zakat* while traveling (and thus in need of resources).[17] The mention of travelers in the hadith is simply an elaboration of the Qur'anic command in relation to wayfarers. Therefore, though a person may possess enough wealth to donate *zakat*, he may also be eligible as a recipient, provided that he is in need during travels.

WHERE ELSE CAN *ZAKAT* BE GIVEN?

The essential aim of *zakat* is to cure all social diseases that stem from inequality in the distribution of wealth and, ultimately, create a tightly knit community resembling a robust building. Evidently, there exist certain institutions which are aimed at serving the exact purpose for which *zakat* is intended, and these tend to be well known within a community. Even though these institutions have technically not been mentioned among the other categories of recipients, they do receive *zakat* owing to their particular social aims and functions. These institutions, which are formed around the core concept of charity, have the power to reach out to the deprived, to ease their lives and, as discussed above, help avoid or discourage potential social strife.

In the words of the Prophet (upon whom be peace), a Muslim society is like one body where all parts join the agony of a single limb; viewed from this angle, reviving one certain part of society is commensurable to breathing new life into the entire organism. Espousing this kind of an impetus, each member of society is expected to become active. Actualizing God's will in all parts of society will, in effect, terminate theft and other crimes connected to financial instability, graciously giving the community a brand new lease on life. While charity and aid foundations, scholarship funds and orphanages may, at first, give the impression of being excluded from the eight groups delineated by the Qur'an, they each fundamentally relate and encompass one or more of the specified recipient groups. The dictates of the Qur'an, in effect, are both general and unrestricted— the essence of a vibrant and comprehensive system of ordinances for life. Therefore, conditions like poverty, traveling, being in debt, or striving in the way of God are inherently deemed to generate the need for assistance, so that individuals in such conditions clearly achieve eligibility for *zakat*, and organizations which provide such targeted assistance must receive available funds in order to deliver the appropriate relief.

Illat, in Islamic terminology, means the basic reason for determining the permissibility or the impermissibility of an action, and it constitutes a crucial foundation of Islamic jurisprudence. Recall that as far as the *muallafa al-qulub* are concerned, they receive *zakat* as long as, or whenever and wherever, they exist and there is a need for warming their hearts towards Islam. The situation is similar for wayfarers, as discussed above; namely, *zakat* is only given to such a group as long as it exists—that is, as long as individuals fitting this description can be identified. Therefore, looking from this perspective, we can say that the very existence of institutions or foundations which serve the needs of any of the individuals defined, and which have as their primary intent and purpose the support of these groups, is sufficient reason for their entitlement to *zakat*.

IS PERSONAL TRANSFER (*TAMLIK*) A REQUIREMENT?

Following this discussion of the Qur'an's unequivocal exposition of the eight groups of recipients for *zakat*, the issue of *tamlik* (the process of handing over the *zakat* to the recipient in person) must be examined. The Hanafi School, especially, has laid great emphasis on the issue, accentuating the necessity of giving the *zakat* in person.

For the recipients to dispose of the *zakat* as they wish, it is imperative that they possess full rights and ownership over it, as discussed above; but further, the *zakat* should be transmitted to the beneficiaries in person in order to guarantee that their needs are met without any outside interference. Otherwise, *zakat's* essential purpose, to act as a bridge between social classes, might not be achieved, due to a preliminary infringement on the right of the recipient. Hence, many scholars have included *tamliq* as an inseparable prerequisite of zakat, obligating the benefactor or an authorized proxy to deliver the *zakat* personally. This ruling has beneficially resulted in the prevention of probable misunderstandings and infringements that might have otherwise occured, as well as clearly having the practice in line with the Islamic spirit.

This requirement of personal transfer, according to the Hanafi School, is predicated upon the direct order to "Pay *zakat*!" Such a command can only be fulfilled by virtue of payment in person to the specified individuals and locations. To realize this task, it is acceptable to give the funds to the specified person, in question, or to the directors or supervisors of charity foundations because, according to Abu Hanifa, the originator of the Hanafi tradition of jurisprudence, the requirement of *tamlik* can simply be fulfilled by ensuring that the *zakat* will ultimately reach its recipients, as is the case with charity funds and foundations.

The words used in the verse in specifying the locations of disbursement are of further importance. While the Arabic preposition used prior to naming the poor, destitute, *zakat* collectors and *muallafa al-qulub* is *"li,"* ("for"), the preposition employed before slaves, debtors, those working in the way of God and wayfarers is *"fi,"* (in).

Some scholars, basing their view on the preposition *"li,"* have emphasized the requirement of personal transfer, but more importantly have stressed that *zakat* can only be given to individuals, thereby excluding all types of institutions.

However, it must be recalled that the other half of the recipients have been mentioned using the preposition of *"fi,"* which opens the door to there being other possibilities and aspects we must consider. For, otherwise, the verse would certainly have followed a consistent pattern and used the same grammar throughout. The groups denoted by *"fi"* are generally renowned for collective work which surpasses individual capabilities. The "way of God" classification, particularly, has a broad scope, encompassing a vast area of application and comprising of a cluster of categories—such as a soldier, student or pilgrim, just to mention a few. Bearing in mind the Prophet's utilization of *zakat* funds in taking care of the needs of the *Suffa* (the gallant seekers of knowledge), the necessity of establishing foundations that provide an ideal environment for bringing up an exemplary generation whose basic needs are covered becomes manifest. Coercing the benefactor to strictly give his *zakat* directly to the poor instead would be tantamount to undermining charity foundations that could otherwise perfectly transfer the *zakat* to those in genuine need; moreover, such an approach spawns from a superficial understanding of the spirit of Islam. As superbly stated by Bediüzzaman Said Nursi, swords have now been replaced by letters, and the vitality of knowledge has gained even a fresher meaning; thus, the heroes carrying the standards of truth, spreading God's message across the globe, those who have sacrificed their entire lives for the arduous pursuit of knowledge, must be sheltered, through supporting and revitalizing the foundations and institutions that provide a supportive environment for these outstanding heroes. In short, by virtue of offering *zakat* to the representatives of these institutions, a person will fulfill the obligation of *zakat* and, in actual fact, taking the current times and situation into particular consideration, will thus undoubtedly do so in the wisest of all ways.

As a fresh means of endeavor, current scholars are predominantly in agreement with regards to using *zakat* funds to establish and revive institutions of assistance. As strange as it may initially seem, even a brief moment of contemplation will divulge the plausibility of the emphasis which many scholars have placed on utilizing *zakat* to set up hospitals, laboratories, media organizations, financial institutions and, most importantly, educational institutions that will enlighten generations with Islam.

Investing *zakat* in this sort of a domain will, at the same time, provide the benefactor with visible fruits, in addition to the everlasting rewards awaiting him in the eternal abode. From this point of view, all institutions established to convey the revivifying Truth of God are essentially included in the category defined as being, "In the way of God;" and their restoration and reinforcement through *zakat* is indubitably an act of perpetual benefit. More precisely, those seeking to fulfill the obligation of *zakat* in the best possible way should assemble their funds in foundations which strive to implement and convey humankind's ethical values, as exemplified by the Qur'an, so that they can use their financial means to participate in the valiant effort to serve humanity—unquestionably, the noblest of all services.

While opting for this alternative, all benefactors must understand that giving *zakat* in person to the representatives of these institutions fulfills the requirement of *tamlik* and, in actual fact, there is no difference between this method and that of giving it to an individual.

Included in Islam's code of action, it must be recalled, is the strong recommendation to take precautions as circumstance demands and even keep and maintain disheartening forces at hand, as attested to by the verse, *"Make ready for them all you can of force"* (Anfal 8:60). Caliph Umar's maintenance of 80,000 horses in two separate districts, while actively another 40,000 horses, is testimony to his thorough understanding of the verse. For this reason, many scholars have included a soldier's supplies and ammunition in the context of "in the way of God," sanctioning the use of *zakat* funds to cover their entire needs. In this case, handing the *zakat* over to the responsible commander, instead of giving it to the soldier personally, will meet the requirement of *tamlik*. Thus, while the benefactor can feel at ease that he has realized his noble obligation of giving in the way of God, the commander or official who acts as a proxy will also bear the honorable task of flawlessly utilizing the money received, in the best possible way, to cover the necessities of the soldiers. Thus, depending on the sort of need, it may not be necessary to hand over the charity to the soldier himself; for instance, small supplies like food or clothes are best given directly to the soldier, whereas larger qualities are better given to the administrators.

SOME ISSUES CONCERNING THE PLACES OF DISBURSEMENT

A. CAN ALL OF ONE'S *ZAKAT* BE GIVEN TO A SINGLE PERSON AT ONCE?

The gathered *zakat* of a person, according to the Shafii school, must be distributed among at least three people belonging to any of the eight specified categories, as the wordings used for each is always plural, insinuating a multiplicity of persons. Hence, the *zakat* must be given to at least three different individuals, though it can certainly be given to more.

The majority, including the Hanafi scholars, insist that the plural wording used in the verse actually simply denotes the multiplicity of specific types, so that *zakat* could be paid to any individual belonging to any of the many categories, regardless of their numbers. According to this school, then, as well as being able to give the entire *zakat* to a single category, the benefactor may also present it to a single person or foundation. Expounding the categories of recipients, the verse leaves the freedom of choice to the benefactor. If we were to take the *li* preposition out of its symbolic context and understand it to pertain to each member of the specified categories, then inevitably, the donor would have to distribute *zakat* among every single person in each of these categories—clearly an impossible task in realistic terms.

In a nutshell, it will suffice to give the *zakat* to any single person or organization, provided that eligibility is established, and there is no need to impose any strictness or particular complications on what is, in fact, a simple task.

B. CAN *ZAKAT* BE GIVEN TO CLOSE RELATIVES?

Insofar as social obligations and issues pertaining to economical life are concerned, Islam has given visible priority to relatives, as testified by God's Command to His Messenger before embarking on the mission to spread His word, *"And warn your tribe of near kindred"* (Shuara 26:214).

The Noble Prophet, applying the monumental ethics and morals extolled by the Qur'an, clearly abided by the verse, commencing with his kin, continually warning them upon the slightest oscillation that their personal relationship with the Prophet would be of no avail if they were ever to lead a life outside the borders laid down by God.

When the verse, *"You will not attain righteousness until you spend of what you love"* (Al Imran 3:92) was revealed, the Prophet refused Abu Talha's desire to donate his entire garden at "Beyruha," advising him to distribute it among his relatives instead. On one occasion, when a female Companion conveyed the view of her husband and son concerning *sadaqa*, the Messenger of God declared, "Your husband, Ibn Masud, and your son have spoken the truth. The best charity you can ever offer is towards them."[18] This amplifies the importance of donating to kin. The Prophet, in a similar fashion, advised another relatively poor Companion to observe the following order in charity, "Start from yourself; if there is any left over, give to your family; then to your relatives; then so on and so on (basically to everybody else)."[19]

In another hadith, the Prophet (upon whom be peace) elaborates, "*Sadaqa* given to a destitute acquires one reward, whereas *sadaqa* given to relatives acquires two."[20]

Supplementary evidence can also be put forth to corroborate this systematic order of charity established by the Prophet. The basic issue, however, is simple: the natural sequence of lineage as well as such institutions as charity and aid foundations, scholarship funds and orphanages around the donor should be kept in mind, and observed equitably in the matter of *zakat*.

C. IN OUR DAY, WHAT ARE THE BEST PLACES TO GIVE *ZAKAT*?

The most virtuous act can differ according to place and time. A certain act, appropriate at one time, may lose its status in another. During a time, for instance, the most virtuous act was *hijra* (the abandoning of the home country and all possessions and migrating for God and His Prophet), an immense sacrifice whose virtues have been announced by the Prophet (upon whom be peace). *Hijra*, in its full sense of the term, then meant the display of a Muslim's perseverance in the face of non-believers and his efforts, both individual and collective, to reinforce Islam. At other times, however, upon being asked to identify the most virtuous acts, the Honorable Prophet gave alternative responses, like *salat* performed on time, struggling in the way of God, or upholding high morals—implying that certain acts may outshine others depending on the person, time or place.

From the very beginning, scholars have put focus on the need to establish what constitutes the most virtuous place for disbursement, with some believing that it would be best to offer it to all the eight groups at once, with others laying more emphasis on some groups over others. Be that as it may, the bottom line is that the state of virtue differs according to various cases and needs, thus the underlying factor in divergent scholarly interpretations should be sought according to the particular conditions at the time, and place, in which one lives.

At this point, it will be of immense benefit to highlight certain aspects which are helpful in determining the most ideal places for disbursement. The essential consideration, as always, is that with the assistance of *zakat*, social and economical deficiencies should be repaired. Obviously, it is also important that *zakat* not be senselessly frittered away; on the contrary, all efforts should be coalesced in the mission to patch up social wounds. Uniting all efforts by collecting every single drop into one gigantic basin will providentially provide the means for the mental and intellectual enlightenment of aspiring minds, as well as satisfying the appetite of those hungry for Truth.

Indeed, it is great to give to the poor or destitute; and it is also highly commendable to reach out to students, who are themselves prone to becoming victims of insidious movements and falling into the destructive traps of sinister ideologies. Thus, today's Muslims need to seek to utilize their *zakat* for the common good, in the name of securing a future for Islam. Effectively lending full support to well-founded institutions and organizations which strive to create, for these students, prosperously blissful and harmonious environments, will ensure their development into constructive and productive characters who are able to assume their own responsibilities for the perpetuation of *zakat* and the health of new generations and communities. Indubitably, our most vital duty is to provide a haven for a generation on the edge of becoming devoid of thought and values and to construct an inner spirituality in them, assuring them a place as architects of the future. Establishing educational institutions which are home to remarkable teaching remains one of the best ways to accomplish this ideal—and thus the relative advisability of mobilizing *zakat* funds for such a purpose becomes self-evident.

It must always be kept in mind that each period of time harbors its own unique problems and priorities, as exemplified by the Noble Prophet's alternating emphases on acts like pilgrimage, kindness to parent, *salat* offered on time, and many other financial or physical demonstrations of faith—all of which all are undoubtedly highly virtuous. Thus, the concept of striving efficiently in the way of God must be re-examined, keeping the current state of world affairs close at hand. For the Arabic term *jihad* (striving) encompasses every kind of struggle and effort which is exerted in the way of God. As a result, even cultural activities may be considered to be striving in that they are essential pursuits which bind the community of believers to one another and result in substantial and permanent social effects and impressions.

At this point in human history, we face the enemy in ignorance—an adversary which can only be crushed through a resuscitation of knowledge of God, or gnosis. Thus, reminding ourselves and others about belief, enjoining good, and forbidding evil all become critically incumbent duties on all Muslims. We must all reach the important realization that the world today is in desperate need of sound Islamic teachings, perhaps more than it has ever been. In the words of Bediüzzaman Said Nursi, if we had been perfectly successful in representing Islam's essentials and ideals, the members of other affiliations would have entered the fold of Islam in masses by now. It is unfortunate but true that our failure to truly communicate the beauty of Islam—both explicitly, in our words and teachings, and implicitly, in the models of humanity we present as ourselves—has been equally matched by the seeming apathy of much of the world in seeking the path to salvation. If Muslims sincerely aspire to solve this problem, they must establish and bolster such foundations and foster and nurture our future, most especially the youth. And this will only be accomplished through collective and concerted efforts to channel the bulk of resources towards the proper education of the younger generation.

D. WHO CANNOT BE GIVEN *ZAKAT*?

Zakat is a financial deed whose benefactors and recipients have unequivocally been specified. In addition to declaring all the eight eligible categories, the essential references of Islam—Qur'an and Sunna—have also identified the groups which are not entitled to *zakat*.

In enumerating the two deeds that are truly worthy of envy (not to be understood in its negative sense), the Prophet (upon whom be peace) includes the person who "constantly donates to where merited, to the point of insolvency,"[21] an allusion to the inappropriateness of giving *zakat* or *sadaqa* to undeserving people or places.

Put in a nutshell, people ineligible to receive *zakat* can be enumerated as the rich; those who have the power and ability to work; and intimate relatives or progeny of the Noble Prophet (upon whom be peace). Let's now scrutinize each of these categories in light of the respective evidence.

1. The rich

The rich are obliged to give *zakat*, not to receive it, as attested to by the hadith, "*Sadaqa* is not permissible for the rich (to receive);"[22] equally, the Prophet's advice to Muadh before dispatching him to Yemen attests: "It (wealth) is taken from the rich and given to the poor."[23]

In another hadith, the Prophet (upon whom be peace) forewarned, "A person who asks of others, despite possessing enough wealth for sustenance, will be brought on the Day of Judgment with his face scarred by his demands as if it had been scraped with nails." In answer to subsequent inquiries about what could be considered "enough wealth," his answer was "50 *dirhams*."[24] Furthermore, the Messenger unambiguously stated, "*Sadaqa* is not permissible for whoever is wealthy with the power to work."[25]

The general exclusion of the rich from *zakat* notwithstanding, there are some who have been identified as being eligible to receive it, as justified by the subsequent hadith, wherein the Prophet included certain among the rich in those eight categories: "Charity is not permissible for the rich, except for the following five: a warrior in the way of God, a *zakat* collector, a debtor, a person who buys the charity collected as *zakat*, and a rich person who receives from a poor the gift that was given to him as *zakat*."[26]

Officially wealthy children or a female, regardless of whether or not they exercise authority over their possessions, are also ineligible to receive *zakat*, since a female with a wealthy husband or the child of a rich father is also classified as being rich because Islam has obliged the male—whether it be the father or husband—with the duty of providing her sustenance. By the same token, *zakat* cannot be given to the children under the financial protection of a wealthy guardian.

2. Those with the power to work

Islam does not condone supporting those who, although they possess enough ability and power, adamantly insist on leading a parasitical life; contrarily, the Qur'an praises and emphasizes personal effort and toil, as accentuated by the verse: *"...and that each can have nothing save what he strives for"* (Najm 53:39).

In a hadith overruling the eligibility of those with the power to work, the Prophet declared that, *"Sadaqa* is not permissible for a wealthy person or for one with the power to work."[27] The Prophet extols personal effort in another hadith:

> A man from among the *Ansar* (Medinan Companions) came to the Prophet (upon whom be peace) and begged from him. He (the Prophet) asked, "Have you nothing in your house?" He replied, "Yes, a piece of cloth, a part of which we wear and a part of which we spread (on the ground), and a wooden bowl from which we drink water." He said, "Bring both to me." He then brought these articles to him and he (the Prophet) took them in his hands and asked those present, "Who will buy these?" A man said, "I shall buy them for one *dirham*." The Prophet said, "Who will offer more than one *dirham*?" Another man said, "I shall buy them for two *dirhams*." He (the Prophet) gave these to him and took the two dirhams and, giving them to the *Ansar*, he said, "God and buy food for your family with one *dirham*, and with another buy an axe and bring it to me." He then brought it to him. The Messenger of God fixed a handle on it with his own hands and said, "Go, gather firewood, sell it and meet me after 15 days." The man went away, cut wood and sold

it. When he had earned ten *dirhams*, he came to him and bought a garment with some of them and food with the others. The Messenger of God (upon whom be peace) then said, "This is better for you than that begging should come as a spot on your face on the Day of Judgment."[28]

Notwithstanding the view of some scholars who advise donors to give *zakat* to persons simply according to outward appearances because of the utter impossibility of knowing another's status with certitude, many scholars are adamantly against giving *zakat* to a person who may be considered "an idler." Ideally, it is perhaps better to initially offer them assistance via *zakat*, and thus give them an opportunity to stand on their own, an approach that will, in time, effectively discern between the hard workers and freeloaders.

3. Warring non-Muslims

Withholding *zakat* from those in active warfare against Muslims is a verdict that is established by both Islamic sources and logical thinking, in addition to the consensus of scholars. The Almighty has explicitly declared, *"God only forbids you to make friends with those who have fought against you on account of your religion and driven you from your homes, or abetted others to do so"* (Mumtahina 60:9). This clearly dictates the code of conduct to be embraced against those with obstinate hatred, who incessantly and publicly strive to thwart the splendor of Islam.

This is actually what common sense calls for, as lending financial support to those preparing to engage in hostilities would practically be tantamount to self-destruction. Even though such a donation might be considered to stimulate peace, this would certainly be a highly strategic decision, in need of meticulous planning and a great deal of preliminary thought.

As made palpable by the verse, the group in question refers to non-Muslims who have made a habit of callously attacking and assaulting Muslims—not to be confused with the minorities living in Muslim realms who, as verified by the consensus of the scholars, may at least be given supererogatory *sadaqa* if in need. It is a well-known fact that Caliph Umar had even allotted a salary from the treasury for an aged non-Muslim lady. Concurrently, this sort of benevolence is necessitated by the teachings Islam promulgates in the name of humanity. Exemplified by the *muallafa al-qulub* charity, heart-warming grants like these are providentially the means for many to bear witness to the positives of life, a scene that may well culminate in the precious result of the acceptance of Islam.

4. Intimate family members

A person cannot give *zakat* to those he is obliged to look after, who include his *usul* (origin and progeny), namely parents and children, but exclude the *furu* (other relatives). Giving *zakat* to parents or children will not realize the profound goal of *zakat*, causing wealth to continuously change only between the same hands, a procedure prohibited by the Qur'an: *"...so that they will not become the property of the rich among you"* (Hashr 59:7). Equally, this is equivalent to using *zakat* money to close a debt in that the sustenance of parents and children is commensurate with a debt awaiting payment.

Insofar as grandparents and grandchildren are concerned, scholars have opted for both sides of the issue, stemming from different categorizations as either *usul* or *furu*. While some maintain their ineligibility due to their inclusion as *usul*, other scholars insist on their eligibility as *furu*, granting the responsibility on both occasions to the father.

As for giving *zakat* to other relatives, it is considered not only acceptable but commendable, and a means of strengthening community bonds through *sila al-rahim* (the reinforcement of relational ties). Thus it is said to acquire double the rewards, as attested to by the assurance of the Prophet (upon whom be peace) in the following hadith: "A *sadaqa* given to a destitute is one *sadaqa*, whereas a *sadaqa* given to relatives is *sadaqa* and *sila al-rahim*."[29] The Noble Messenger's advice to Abu Talha and Sa'd ibn Abi Waqqas spawns from this exact approach, recommending to them, on behalf of the entire Muslim community, that it is much more appropriate to give priority in charity and alms to family and relatives, lest they become dependent on others.

5. The descendents of the Prophet

The progeny of the Noble Messenger, collectively known as *Bani Hashim* (the children of Hashim), are equally ineligible to be *zakat* recipients. Shafii, contrary to the opinions of Abu Hanifa, Malik and Ibn Hanbal, further extends this boundary by similarly integrating the children of Abd al-Muttalib, the Prophet's grandfather. So, accordingly, the Prophet's (upon whom be peace) relatives comprise his own family, plus the families of Aqil, Jafar, Abbas and Haris.

The Prophet had once appointed a man from the tribe of *Bani Mahzun* to collect charity, who had then asked Abu Rafi, a former slave emancipated by *Bani Hashim*, to join him, so as to acquire a share of it. Upon hearing this, the Messenger proclaimed, "An emancipated slave of a tribe is a member of it, and certainly *sadaqa* is not held (allowed) for us."[30] When Hasan, the grandson of the Prophet, reached out to a date given in charity, the Prophet prevented him by saying, "You should know that we do not eat of *zakat*."[31] Likewise, the Prophet (upon whom be peace) had said, "Time and again when I return to my abode, I come across a date fallen on my bed; and as soon as I seize the date for consumption, I drop it in fear it may be *sadaqa*."[32]

On top of prohibiting his family members and relatives from charity and alms, the Prophet (upon whom be peace) equally did not consent to them working as *zakat* collectors, a profession that entailed a compulsory receival of *zakat*. Nonetheless, he did authorize for himself and his family a portion of one-fifth of the gains of war that was entitled to him, in addition to the gifts he had received.

The eighth chapter of the Qur'an begins by emphasizing the basic principle that the gains of war belong to God and His Messenger, "*They (the believers) ask you about the gains of war. Say: "The war-gains belong to God and the Messenger,*" (Anfal 8:1) and then clarifies the how the gains of war will be distributed, *"And know that whatever you take as gains of war, to God belongs one fifth of it, and to the Messenger, and the near kinsfolk, and orphans, and the destitute, and the wayfarer (one devoid of sufficient means of journeying)"* (Anfal 8:41). This verse assigns one-fifth to God first, that is to public services by mentioning the people who represent these services: the Messenger, his near kinsfolk, orphans, the destitute and the wayfarer who does not have sufficient means to complete the journey. The remainder is distributed among the warriors.

The Messenger (upon whom be peace) devoted all his life to communicating Islam to others and to the service of the people. He was not in a position to provide for the poor among his kinsfolk. In addition, there were many other places or items of expenditure for which the Messenger had to pay as both a Messenger and the head of the state. The share assigned to him may, in some respects, be likened to the funds assigned for the special expenditure of heads of state.

It is a historical fact that the Messenger, upon him be peace and blessings, spent his first wife Khadija's wealth on the cause of calling to Islam, while he, his family and his kinsfolk lived as the poorest of all Muslims. They also spent all the shares of the gains of war that were assigned to them on Islamic services and the needy.

It has also been narrated that the Prophet would investigate the source of each gift and would then use it only if and when its legitimacy had been confirmed; if such could not be established, he simply transferred the alms or charity to others, or returned it back to the *Bayt al-Mal* (treasury).

CHAPTER 7

Sadaqa al-Fitr

CHARITIES APART FROM *ZAKAT*

Factors of economic revitalization, in Islam, are not reserved just to *zakat*. In fact, the *sadaqa al-fitr* (charity of fast breaking), sacrifice, *aqiqa* (sacrifice offered in celebration and gratitude of a newborn child), *walima* (the wedding feast), *eid* (religious festival), *nazr* (votive offering), *wasiyya* (will), and *waqf* (a charity foundation), while enumerated among economic activities are also acts that acquire a spiritual proximity with God. Among other additional points worth noticing are the compensations and fines imposed on those who, as part of human nature, commit the occasional discrepancies, including the fines for the arbitrary annulment of fasting, for violated vows, and for the illegalities pertaining to pilgrimage—not to mention the hefty compensation for mistakenly killing someone. In addition, when the supererogatory charities avidly encouraged by the Qur'an and Sunna, regardless of time and place, are brought to mind, the absolute breadth and depth of Islamic tenets aimed at solving the problem of destitution, while upholding the essential dignity of the poor, become crystal clear.

The generalization of Qur'anic declarations that encourage *sadaqa* accentuates the fact that it carries no limitations whatsoever.

> Say: "Indeed my Lord enlarges the provision for whom He wills of His servants, and narrows it (for whom He wills). And whatsoever you spend for good He replaces it. And He is the Best of Providers." (Saba 34:39)

> Whatever good thing you spend, it is for your own soul and you shall do so only for God's sake. And whatever good you

> spend, it will be repaid to you in full and you will not be wronged." (Baqara 2:272)

> And whatever good things you spend, surely God knows them well. (Baqara 2:273)

Yet these are just a few corroborative verses that immediately spring to mind.

The Noble Messenger has also drawn attention to the broad extent of the term by the recommendation mentioned earlier, "Save yourselves from hellfire, even if it be with half a date."[1] Furthermore, the glad tidings of the Messenger (upon whom be peace), to the effect that angels hasten their *dua* or well-wishes for those who offer supererogatory *sadaqa* or charity, in addition to the encompassing of God's blessing on their wealth, are all magnificent pretexts for becoming an active part of such a glorious act. This fact will become even more evident if each of these potential sources of power is scrutinized.

THE *SADAQA AL-FITR*

Literally, *fitr* means breaking the fast or creation. The *sadaqa al-fitr*, however, is a financial obligation for Muslims who at the time of the Festivity of Ramadan, possess more than the prescribed amount of provisions for themselves and their dependents after giving the *sadaqa al-fitr.*

Sadaqa al-fitr is *wajib* (necessary) according to the Hanafi School, and *fard* (obligatory) according to other Islamic Schools of Jurisprudence. It is also called the "head *zakat*," owing to the fact that it's a financial responsibility for each person. As for its compulsoriness, technically, it is a display of gratitude upon the first day of the Festivity of Ramadan.

In many hadith, the Prophet of God has commanded the offering of *sadaqa al-fitr*. Ibn Umar, one of the Companions, conveyed the following: "The Messenger of God has decreed *sadaqa al-fitr* compulsory on slaves, men, women, children and adults as a measure of dates and of barley to be given before the eid prayer (the prayer marking the end of Ramadan)."[2] Another narration in relation is that of Abu Said al-Hudri's: "We had given *sadaqa al-fitr* at the time of the Prophet, from our provisions, which were, at the time, barley, raisins, dates and cheese."[3] In another hadith, the following declaration can be cited, "Pay the *sadaqa al-fitr* on behalf of those under your guardianship."[4]

The *sadaqa al-fitr*, as an established deed in Islam, is offered in gratitude for the blessings of life and the existence bestowed by the Creator on a person and on those under his or her care. Indeed, the compulsoriness of *sadaqa al-fitr* is not entailed by fasting; rather, it is compulsory for everyone, regardless of whether they fast or not.

As alluded to by the hadith, *sadaqa al-fitr* mends those ignoble actions, which are undesirable for all of us and quite unacceptable for those who fast, thus virtually completing the month of physical sacrifice while giving the poor grounds and means by which to join in the celebrations of Ramadan Eid.[5] It has also been added that the offering of *sadaqa al-fitr* consolidates the acceptance of fasting, acquires salvation, and grants liberation from the anguish of death and the tribulations of the grave.

DOES *SADAQA AL-FITR* ENCOMPASS A GREATER AREA THAN THAT OF *ZAKAT*?

Sadaqa al-fitr, performed by obligation, encompasses a greater area than that of *zakat* and providentially is a means whereby everybody enjoys the opportunity to taste the heavenly flavor of spending in the way of God. In other words, it allows everyone a way of seeing and comprehending, first hand, the situation of the poor, as well as providing a chance for those with means to learn how to assist the poor without compromising their dignity. Consequently, a robust and permanent bridge of friendship is built between members of society.

WHAT ARE THE REQUIREMENTS FOR
THE OBLIGATION OF *SADAQA AL-FITR*?

Here are the conditions for obligation:

1. BEING A MUSLIM

To be under the obligation of *sadaqa al-fitr*, one needs to be a Muslim. According to the Shafii School, however, a non-Muslim also needs to pay *sadaqa al-fitr* for those Muslims of kindred living under his care.

2. POSSESSING WEALTH EQUIVALENT TO (AT LEAST) NISAB

As it is in *zakat*, to become eligible for *sadaqa al-fitr*, one needs to possess, apart from the basic necessities, wealth equivalent to *nisab*, an amount equal to 85 grams of gold or 595 grams of silver. Unlike *zakat*, the possessed wealth does not need to be of increasing nature and a full year does not need to elapse. The Shafii, Hanbali and Maliki Schools contend that *nisab* is not a pre-requisite for *sadaqa al-fitr*; in fact, every Muslim possessing the basic necessities as well as the sustenance to see him through the night of *Eid* is compelled to perform *sadaqa al-fitr*. A person having become obliged with *sadaqa al-fitr* does not become free of this obligation upon losing his wealth or having it drop below *nisab*. However, if one dies owing *sadaqa al-fitr*, this debt need not to be extracted out of his will, though it is better for the beneficiaries to offer it voluntarily.

3. AHLIYAH (THE RIGHT TO DISPOSE ON PROPERTY OR WEALTH)

Sadaqa al-fitr does not necessitate one to be an *aqil baligh* (i.e. sane adult). Leading Hanafi jurists, Abu Hanifa and Abu Yusuf, maintain that the *sadaqa al-fitr* needs to be given even from the wealth owned by a juvenile or a person who is mentally ill; moreover, a father must give *sadaqa al-fitr* from the possessions of his wealthy child.

4. GUARDIANSHIP AND RESPONSIBILITY OF SUPERVISION

For one to be compelled with the fulfillment of *sadaqa al-fitr* on behalf of others, these others must be under guardianship as people whom one is obliged to take care of. A Muslim, wealthy enough to be eligible for *sadaqa al-fitr* must also offer it for the children and the mentally ill who lack financial resources and are living in his custody, or under his care. Additionally, grandchildren whose father has passed away must also be paid *sadaqa al-fitr* for. In conjunction, however, one is not required to pay *sadaqa al-fitr* for parents, children who have become adults, the wife, brothers and sisters even if they are living under one's care, owing to the fact that they are not technically under his guardianship. Anyhow, one is more than welcome to voluntarily offer fitr for them. However, the majority of scholars, except for the Hanafi, advise that one is required to offer *sadaqa al-fitr* for his Muslim parents and wife living under his care, if in possession of the minimum wealth.

5. TIME

The performance of *sadaqa al-fitr* becomes necessary, according to the Hanafi School, on the first day of Ramadan Eid, with the break of dawn, as *sadaqa al-fitr* is a charity attached with this specific moment in time. Accordingly, if one dies or becomes poor before the dawn of the first day of the Eid, he is no longer compelled with its performance, although offering it is necessary for those who are born or have become Muslim before the dawn of the day. *Sadaqa al-fitr* is not necessary for a baby born after dawn, or for one who has embraced Islam after dawn for that matter. Other Islamic jurisprudential schools hold the view that *sadaqa al-fitr* becomes necessary with the sunset of the final day of Ramadan.

WHEN IS *SADAQA AL-FITR* GIVEN?

Sadaqa al-fitr can be given as soon as Ramadan commences. Scholars, in addition, have recommended its payment at least a couple of days prior to Eid, in accordance with its aim of assisting the poor in acquiring their needs. Delaying its payment until after the first day of Eid is inappropriate. Nonetheless, given that it has been delayed, the obligation continues and thus it must be fulfilled immediately. According to the Shafii School, it is forbidden to delay the payment of fitr, without excuse, until after the first day of Eid.

How much needs to be given?

As mentioned before in the hadiths, *sadaqa al-fitr* had been given during the time of the Noble Prophet from the most common food-stuffs like dates, barley and raisins, in the amount of 1 sa'a (a measurement equivalent to 3.350 kg). In addition, it has been narrated that the companions gave a half a sa'a of wheat as *sadaqa al-fitr*.

Assessing the accounts stated above, scholars have identified the type and amount of *sadaqa al-fitr* as follows. The Hanafi School maintains that *sadaqa al-fitr* can be given from four items of nutrition, namely, wheat, barley, date and raisins, including half a sa'a from wheat, including its flour, and one sa'a from the others. According to Shafii Scholars, fitr is given as one sa'a from all kinds of grain, dates and raisins, although at best, *sadaqa al-fitr* should be given from the most consumed food item in that particular area or country.

This is the information cited in the classical texts of jurisprudence. However, when scrutinizing the application of *sadaqa al-fitr* during the era of the Prophet (upon whom be peace), and keeping in mind its nature and purpose, it becomes evident that fitr, then given as one sa'a, is commensurable with the daily sustenance of the poor. Moreover, what had been offered as fitr were the society's basic items of consumption. Therefore, *sadaqa al-fitr* must have been aimed towards covering the daily (day-night) sustenance of the poor, keeping in mind the social standards at that time. Therefore, it can be argued that in our day, it is no longer sufficient to pay *sadaqa al-fitr* from the listed foodstuffs in the mentioned amounts. In line with these considerations, current Muslim scholars hold the view that the following standards should, instead, be taken as essential criterions in determining *sadaqa al-fitr*.

First, it is important to calculate the monetary average of one sa'a of wheat, barley, dates and raisins in their entirety, whereby the amount is ascertained according to the diverse quality and value of each item, a practice that will prevent inconsistent calculations between Muslims. It is imperative that the adequate amount of daily sustenance per person is taken as a measure, and this amount must not be of lesser value that the food items enumerated in the hadith. Insofar as the true meaning of *sadaqa al-fitr* is concerned, it is more fitting to determine the daily sustenance according to the social standard of the benefactor rather than the recipient. The Qur'anic declaration pertaining to the compensation of unfulfilled vows bolsters this approach: *"...the expiation thereof is the feeding of the needy with average of that which you feed your own people."* (Maidah 5:89)

Furthermore, the measured amount of *sadaqa al-fitr* indicated in various hadith and transmitted in jurisprudential texts is the bare minimum. The real gist of *sadaqa al-fitr*, as alluded to by the Prophet (upon whom be peace) is to prevent the poor, on Eid day, from imploring from others—and to include them, with dignity—in the celebrations of the day.[6] The benefactor must, therefore, determine the amount of *sadaqa al-fitr*, in money, which is required for daily sustenance according to his own economic condition and social standards.

This may be calculated as such: monthly kitchen expenditures are divided by 30, then by the amount of family members; the result will indicate one person's average daily expenses for sustenance within a particular household, the amount to be given as *sadaqa al-fitr*. It is better, however, for Muslims who are financially comfortable to offer even more. God knows best.

How should *SADAQA AL-FITR* be paid?

Sadaqa *al-fitr* is an act of worship, and thus it necessitates the pronouncement of the intention to be uttered upon payment or beforehand, during the allocation of the amount.

Through intention, the heart intends that the *sadaqa al-fitr* is for the sake of God, and though the essence of this intention lays in the heart, it can also be uttered in confirmation. The benefactor should be in a state of mind wherein he recognizes that he is returning to its proper owners the wealth entrusted with him by the Creator—rather than seeing himself or herself as a "generous" person. Thus, there is no need to publicize by saying, "This is *sadaqa al-fitr*," during payment, and there is an important requirement to avoid issuing reminders of one's generosity: *"Cancel not your charity by reminders of your generosity or by injury"* (Baqara 2:264).

In terms of assisting the poor in taking care of their necessities, it is better to offer *sadaqa al-fitr* in cash, although according to need, it may well be paid in the form of the other items. *Sadaqa al-fitr* must be handed over to the poor as bestowed property; critically, therefore, it is not valid for someone to pay *sadaqa al-fitr* in expectation of a repayment.

WHO ARE THE RECIPIENTS OF *SADAQA AL-FITR*?

The locations for disbursing both *sadaqa al-fitr* and *zakat* are the same. Therefore, those ineligible for *zakat* are also ineligible to receive *sadaqa al-fitr*. Those who are not entitled to accept *sadaqa al-fitr* are as follows: people deemed rich by Islam, in other words, those in possession of wealth equivalent to *nisab*, irrespective of it being augmentable or not, the wife of the benefactor, parents and grandparents alike, as well as children, grandchildren and others whom the benefactor is obliged to look after. The benefactor should give priority to the poor within close vicinity, relatives even if they are far, and students. Instead of giving *sadaqa al-fitr* only to one person, the benefactor may choose to distribute it among a few people—although bearing in mind that *sadaqa al-fitr* should ultimately take care of a person's daily sustenance, it is perhaps wiser, or more easily accomplished, to present it to one person. Moreover, *sadaqa al-fitr* collected from a few donors can be given to one single recipient.

CONCLUSION

- *Zakat*, in Islam, is not simply an intangible virtue; rather, it is one of Islam's most essential pillars, one of its greatest principles, and one type of the four acts pertaining to worship. Failing to perform it, therefore, is a great sin, while rejecting its validity is commensurable with heresy. It is certainly not a voluntary charity nor a supererogatory *sadaqa*; it is an obligation deeply rooted in the Divine Command.

- As far as Islam is concerned, *zakat* is the entitled right of the poor in the wealth of the rich, a right preordained by God, the Ultimate and True Owner of all seen and unseen treasures, as incumbent on His wealthy vicegerents. Thus bearing this in mind, it is blatantly inimical to common sense for the rich to use *zakat* as a pretext for disdaining the poor, as it would be for a teller to scorn the people he is handing out money to, on the order of his boss.

- *Zakat* is a specified right, with a prescribed time, minimum amount, prerequisites, benefactors and recipients—all thoroughly articulated by Islam in order to smooth the progress of its fulfillment by its adherents.

- This duty is not left to the conscience alone; on the contrary, the Islamic government is obligated with its impartial collection and distribution via *zakat* collectors. *Zakat* is not just a charity; rather, it is more of a Divine Tax. For this reason, the verse which relates, *"Take alms from their wealth"* is clearly perceived to be a command, as corroborated by the hadith, "It (*zakat*) is taken from the rich."

- The government is entitled to inflict a punishment on the rejecters of *zakat* to the extent of seizing half their property, as verified by the hadith: "...and we will seize half his property."

– It is an undeniable right of the *imam* (faith leader) or president, etc. to relentlessly combat those who refuse to pay *zakat*, a right explicated by numerous hadiths and exemplified by the unyielding attitude of Caliph Abu Bakr.

– If the government remains indifferent to the duty of collecting *zakat*, or if the society is unconcerned with observing this duty, then it is incumbent on every individual, initially, to realize their personal duties of *zakat* and then strive toward reinstating this vital obligation within the community. *Zakat*, before anything, is an act of worship that brings a person closer to God and purifies the self and subsequently the wealth. Thus, if the government does not enforce it, belief in God and the Qur'an certainly do.

– The revenues of *zakat* are not left to the control of clerics, nor to the desires of administrators and recipients in general; conversely, it is the Qur'an and the Sunna of the Noble Prophet (peace and blessings be upon him) that have palpably specified its benefactors and recipients. Because the process of its distribution is just as vital as its collection, each group of beneficiaries has additionally been thoroughly categorized, leaving nothing in the dark.

– *Zakat* is not a simple assistance consisting of merely taking temporary care of the needs of the poor, then swiftly abandoning them to struggle in the throes of destitution. Instead, *zakat's* splendid aim is to hold the poor by the hand, financially elevating them to becoming, in time, *zakat* donors themselves.

– *Zakat*, identified and elaborated by both the Qu'ran and the Sunna, seeks to realize immense spiritual, ethical, social and political goals, insofar as its places of disbursement are concerned. A comprehensive analysis of the goals and realm of *zakat* will resoundingly testify to its overwhelming superiority to other previous and current notions of alm collection and charity.

NOTES

CHAPTER 1
WHAT IS *ZAKAT*?

1   Ibn Manzur, *Lisan al-Arab*, 14:358.
2   Shams 91:9.
3   A'la 87:14.
4   Maryam 19:13.
5   Kahf 18:19.
6   Ibn Abi Shayba, *Musannaf*, 1:57.
7   Baqara 2:232; Nur 24:28.
8   Kahf 18:19.
9   Maryam 19:19.
10 Kahf 18:74.
11 Jurjani, *Ta'rifat*, 114.
12 Ibn Manzur, *Lisan al-Arab*, 10:193.
13 Yusuf 12:18.
14 Tawba 8:60.
15 Bukhari, *Zakat*, 30.
16 Muslim, *Iman*, 136.
17 Konavi, *Anis al-Fuqaha*, 193.
18 Ibn Manzur, *Lisan al-Arab*, 14:357-8.
19 Bukhari, *Buyu*, 26; Muslim, *Musaqat*, 131.
20 Jurjani, *Ta'rifat*, 39.
21 Ibn Manzur, *Lisan al-Arab*, 4:570.
22 Saba 34:45.
23 *See* Ibn Kathir, *al-Bidaya* 5:4-5.
24 *See* Bukhari, *Wasaya* 3,4; *Manaqib al-Ansar* 49; Muslim, *Wasiyya*, 5-7.
25 *See* Kahf 18:81; Maryam 19:13.
26 *See* Maryam 19:31; Anbiya 21:73; A'raf 7:156.
27 *See* Mu'minun 23:4; Naml 27:3; Luqman 31:4.
28 Rum 30:39.
29 Fussilat 41:67.
30 An'am 6:141.
31 *Musnad*, 1, 461.
32 Ibn Hajar, *Fath al-Bari*, 3, 171.

33 *See* Ahzab 33:33; Baqara 2:43, 83, 110; Nisa 4:77; Hajj 22:78; Nur 24:57; Mujadila 58:13; Muzammil 73:20.

34 *See* Baqara 2:3, 277; Maida 5:55; Anfal 8:3; Tawba 9:5, 11, 18, 71; Naml 27:3; Luqman 31:4; Bayyina 97:5.

35 Baqara 2:177; Tawba 9:18.

36 Maida 5:12.

37 Ra'd 13:22; Fatir 35:29; Anfal 8:3.

38 Tawba 9:103.

39 Tawba 9:60.

40 Refer, for instance, to the Arabic dictionary *Mu'jam al-Mufahras* in reference to the words *zakat* and *sadaqa*.

41 Bukhari, *Iman*, 36; Muslim, *Iman*, 1,5,7.

42 Bukhari, *Iman*, 53; *Zakat*, 1.

43 Bukhari, *Zakat*, 62, 40; Muslim, *Iman*, 29, 31.

44 Muslim, *Iman*, 6.

45 Bukhari, *Ilm*, 6.

46 Bukhari, *Iman*, 1, 3; Muslim, *Iman*, 19-22.

47 Muslim, *Iman*, 36; Bukhari, *Iman*, 17.

48 Abu Dawud, *Ilm*, 2; *Musnad*, 4, 136.

49 Bukhari, *Buyu*, 15.

50 Bukhari, *Zakat*, 50; Muslim, *Zakat*, 107; Tirmidhi, *Zakat*, 107.

51 Muslim, *Zakat*, 108.

52 Bukhari, *Adab*, 27; Muslim, *Birr*, 66.

53 *See* Ibn Hisham, *Sira*, 4, 135-6.

54 *See* Bukhari, *Ilm*, 32; *Libas*, 59; Abu Dawud, *Salat*, 242.

55 *See* Tawba 9:60.

56 *See* Bukhari, *Zakat*, 40, 62; Muslim, *Iman*, 29, 31.

57 Bukhari, *Ahkam*, 17; Muslim, *Zakat*, 110-112.

58 Abu Dawud, *Zakat*, 5.

59 *Musnad*, 1, 204.

60 Bukhari, *Zakat*, 68; Muslim, *Imara*, 26.

61 Muslim, *Zakat*, 167-8; Abu Dawud, *Imara*, 20.

62 *Musnad*, 1, 204.

63 Bayhaqi, *Sunan*, 4, 157.

64 Bayhaqi, *Sunan*, 4, 158.

65 Bayhaqi, *Sunan*, 4, 158.

66 Bukhari, *Ahkam*, 17; Muslim, *Zakat*, 112.

67 *Musnad*, 4, 490.

68 Ibn Maja, *Zakat*, 14.

[69] Bukhari, *Zakat*, 1, 40; *I'tisam*, 2; *Musnad*, 1, 19.

[70] Ibn al-Athir, *al-Kamil*, 2, 161.

[71] Ibn Maja, *Zakat*, 14.

[72] Ibn Hashim, *al-Sirat al-Nabawiyya*, 4, 4.

[73] Ibn al-Athir, *al-Kamil*, 3, 159.

[74] Ibn al-Athir, *al-Kamil*, 3, 159.

[75] Bukhari, *Zakat*, 8; Muslim, *Zakat*, 58.

[76] Bukhari, *Zakat*, 8; Muslim, *Zakat*, 59.

[77] Bukhari, *Zakat*, 8; Muslim, *Zakat*, 61.

[78] Ibn Kathir, *al-Bidaya*, 9, 208-9.

[79] Bukhari, *Iman*, 1; Muslim, *Iman*, 19-21.

[80] Bukhari, *Iman*, 17; *I'tisam*, 28; Muslim, *Iman*, 36.

CHAPTER 2
WHAT ARE THE BENEFITS OF *ZAKAT*?

[1] Bukhari, *Riqaq*, 38; *Musnad*, 6, 256.

[2] Tirmidhi, *Birr*, 40.

[3] Ali al-Muttaqi, *Kanz al-Ummal*, 6, 347.

[4] Abu Dawud, *Zakat*, 46.

[5] Abu Dawud, *Adab*, 66; Tirmidhi, *Birr*, 16.

[6] Munawi, *Fayz al-Qadr*, 1, 464.

[7] Ibn Maja, *Fitan*, 22.

[8] Muslim, *Zakat*, 167-8; Abu Dawud, *Imara*, 20.

[9] Abu Dawud, *Zakat*, 32.

[10] Muslim, *Zakat*, 167-8; Abu Dawud, *Imara*, 20.

[11] Muslim, *Birr*, 69.

[12] Haythami, *Majma al-Zawaid*, 3, 63.

[13] Muslim, *Zakat*, 36-7.

[14] Muslim, *Zakat*, 63; Tirmidhi, *Zakat*, 28.

[15] Bukhari, *Zakat*, 27; Muslim, *Zakat*, 57.

[16] Muslim, *Zuhd*, 3; Tirmidhi, *Zuhd*, 31.

[17] Muslim, *Zuhd*, 3-4.

[18] Muslim, *Zakat*, 24, 26-7.

[19] Muslim, *Zakat*, 28.

[20] *See* Bukhari, *Zakat*, 3.

[21] Baykhaki, *Sunan*, 4:82-3.

[22] Abu Davud, *Zakat*, 4.

[23] Baykhaki, *Sunan*, 4:84.

24 Hakim, *Mustadraq*, 1:390.

25 Tirmidhi, *Zakat*, 2.

26 Bukhari, *Riqaq*, 10; Muslim, *Zakat*, 116-9.

27 Bukhari, *Riqaq*, 6; Muslim, *Zakat*, 13-5.

28 Bukhari, *Zakat*, 64; Muslim, *Zakat*, 176.

29 Bukhari, *Zakat*, 27; Muslim, *Zakat*, 57.

30 Bukhari, *Zakat*, 23.

31 Bukhari, *Zakat*, 10; Muslim, *Zakat*, 66-8.

32 Bukhari, *Badu'l-Wahy*, 1; Muslim, *Iman*, 252.

33 Ibn Hisham, *Sirat al-Nabawiyya*, 2:11.

34 Bukhari, *Jihad*, 70; *Rikak*, 10; Ibn Maja, *Zuhd*, 8.

35 Alluding to the hadith "Insure your wealth through zakat, and cure your ill through medical treatment," see Haythami, *Majma al-Zawaid*, 3:63.

36 The intented hadith cited in al-Muttaqi's *Kanz al-Ummal* 6:525 is, "The damage on property, in the land and in the sea, is due to withholding *zakat*. Therefore, protect your properties with *zakat*."

37 See *Kanz al-Ummal*, 6:296.

38 See Fussilat 41:7.

39 Tirmidhi, *Zuhd*, 3.

40 Bukhari, *Wasaya*, 9; *Zakat*, 18; Muslim, *Zakat*, 94; *Musnad*, 2:4.

41 Gülen, M. Fethullah, *Muhammad: The Messenger of God*, 107.

42 Haythami, *Majma al-Zawaid*, 3:62.

43 Ajluni, *Kashf al-Khafa*, 2:64.

44 Muslim, *Birr wa's Sila*, 32.

45 Ibn Maja, *Sadaqat*, 19.

46 See Qur'an chapters Maida 5:12; Hadid 57:11; Muzammil 73:20.

47 Muslim, *Hajj*, 147; Abu Dawud, *Manasik*, 56.

48 Tirmidhi, *Sifat al-Qiyama*, 60

49 Yazir, *Hak Dini Kur'an Dili*, 5:3148.

50 Canan, *Kutub al-Sitta*, 17:264.

51 Bukhari, *Buyu*, 11.

52 Abu Dawud, *Buyu*, 113; Tirmidhi, *Buyu*, 2.

CHAPTER 3
POSSESSIONS THAT ARE SUBJECT TO *ZAKAT*

1 Muslim, *Zakat* 24.

2 Bukhari, *Zakat*, 32; Tirmidhi, *Zakat*, 3.

3 Abu Ubayd, *Amwal*, 1167.

4   Nasai, *Ziynat*, 39.
5   Abu Dawud, *Zakat*, 3.
6   *See* Bukhari, *Tafsir Sura*, 9; Muslim, *Tawba*, 53-4.
7   *See* Bukhari, *Zakat*, 33; Abu Dawud, *Zakat*, 4; Nasai, *Zakat*, 5.
8   *See* Tirmidhi, *Zakat*, 5; Abu Dawud, *Zakat*, 4.
9   *See* Tirmidhi, *Zakat*, 4; Abu Dawud, *Zakat*, 4; Ibn Maja, *Zakat*, 9.
10   Muslim, *Zakat*, 8, 9; Tirmidhi, *Zakat*, 8.
11   Marginani, *Hidaya*, 1:100.
12   Tirmidhi, *Zakat*, 9.
13   *See* Abu Dawud, *Zakat*, 12.
14   Ibn Maja, *Zakat*, 20.
15   Bukhari, *Zakat*, 55.
16   Bukhari, *Zakat*, 65.

CHAPTER 4
WHO IS OBLIGED WITH *ZAKAT*?

1   *See* Bukhari, *Faraid*, 4, 15, 25a; Muslim, *Faraid*, 14; Tirmidhi, *Janaiz*, 69; Nasai, *Janaiz*, 67.
2   Bukhari, *Talaq*, 11; Abu Dawud, *Hudud*, 17.

CHAPTER 5
HOW IS *ZAKAT* PAID?

1   Bukhari, *Zakat*, 69.
2   *See* Abu Dawud, *Zakat*, 14.
3   *See* Bukhari, *Zakat*, 25; Abu Dawud, *Zakat*, 44.
4   *See* Bukhari, *Zakat*, 24; Abu Dawud, *Zakat*, 11.
5   *See* Abu Dawud, *Zakat*, 43.
6   Muslim, *Zakat*, 80.
7   Muslim, *Zakat*, 91; Bukhari, *Zakat*, 13.
8   Tirmidhi, *Zakat*, 5.
9   Bukhari, *Adhan*, 29; Muslim, *Masajid*, 251.
10   Bukhari, *Zakat*, 55; Abu Dawud, *Zakat*, 12.
11   Muslim, *Zakat*, 42-3.
12   Bukhari, *Zakat*, 8; Muslim, *Zakat*, 63-4.
13   Abu Dawud, *Zakat*, 17.
14   *Tecrid-i Sarih Tercemesi* (Annotated Translation of *Tajrid al-Sarih*), 4:199.

[15] Tirmidhi, *Zakat*, 28.

[16] *See* Tirmidhi, *Zakat*, 37.

[17] Bukhari, *Zakat*, 11.

[18] Ibn Maja, *Wasaya*, 4; *Musnad*, 4:210.

[19] Bukhari, *Zakat*, 34.

[20] Bukhari, *Zakat*, 59; Abu Dawud, *Zakat*, 10.

[21] Abu Dawud, *Zakat*, 4; Nasai, *Zakat*, 4.

[22] Bukhari, *Zakat*, 3; Muslim, *Zakat*, 26; Muwatta, *Jihad*, 3; Abu Dawud, *Zakat*, 32; Nasai, *Zakat*, 2.

[23] Muslim, *Zakat*, 24.

CHAPTER 6
WHERE IS *ZAKAT* GIVEN?

[1] Muslim, *Zakat*, 102; see also Abu Dawud, *Zakat*, 24.

[2] Bukhari, *Zakat*, 41.

[3] Bukhari, *Zakat*, 67.

[4] Bukhari, *Zakat*, 41, Tirmidhi, *Zakat*, 6.

[5] Muslim, *Zakat*, 29; Abu Dawud, *Zakat*, 5.

[6] Muslim, *Zakat*, 177; Abu Dawud, *Zakat*, 5.

[7] Tirmidhi, *Zakat*, 18.

[8] *See* Ibn Hisham, *Sira*, 4:135; Ibn Hajar, *al-Isaaba*, 2:187; Tirmidhi, *Zakat*, 30.

[9] Muslim, *Fadail*, 57.

[10] Bukhari, *Iman*, 22; *Itq*, 15; *Adab*, 44; Muslim, *Ayman*, 40; Abu Dawud, *Adab*, 133; Tirmidhi, *Birr*, 29.

[11] *See* Hujurat 49:13.

[12] Abu Dawud, *Zakat*, 25.

[13] Tirmidhi, *Zakat*, 24.

[14] Bukhari, *Ilm*, 42; Muslim, *Fadail al-Sahaba*, 159.

[15] *See* Bukhari, *Fadail al-Ashab*, 10.

[16] Bayhaqi, *Shuab al-Iman*, 7:314; Daylami, *Musnad*, 5:348.

[17] Abu Dawud, *Zakat*, 22.

[18] Bukhari, *Zakat*, 44.

[19] Muslim, *Zakat*, 41.

[20] Tirmidhi, *Zakat*, 26.

[21] Bukhari, *Zakat*, 5.

[22] Abu Dawud, *Zakat*, 25.

[23] Bukhari, *Zakat*, 1.

24 Tirmidhi, *Zakat*, 22.

25 Tirmidhi, *Zakat*, 23.

26 Abu Dawud, *Zakat*, 25.

27 Tirmidhi, *Zakat*, 23.

28 Abu Dawud, *Sunan*, 1637.

29 Tirmidhi, *Zakat*, 26.

30 Abu Dawud, *Zakat*, 30; Tirmidhi, *Zakat*, 25.

31 Bukhari, *Zakat*, 60; Muslim, *Zakat*, 161.

32 Muslim, *Zakat*, 164-5; Abu Dawud, *Zakat*, 30.

CHAPTER 7
SADAQA AL-FITR

1 Bukhari, *Zakat*, 10; *Adab*, 35; Muslim, *Zakat*, 66-7.

2 Bukhari, *Zakat*, 76; Muslim, *Zakat*, 12.

3 Bukhari, *Zakat*, 74.

4 Bayhaqi, *Sunan al-Qubra*, 4:161.

5 Abu Dawud, *Zakat*, 17.

6 Bayhaqi, *Sunan al-Qubra*, 4:175.

BIBLIOGRAPHY

Abu Dawud, Sulaiman ibn al-Sijistani, *Sunan al-Abu Dawud*, Istanbul: al-Maktabat al-Islamiyya, undated.

Abu Ubayd, al-Qasim ibn Sallam, (ed.: H. Muhammad Harrad), *Kitab al-Amwal*, Cairo, 1969.

Ajluni, Ismail ibn Muhammad, *Kashf al-Khafa wa Muzil al-Libas*, Beirut: Kutub al-Ilmiyya, 1988.

Hanbal, Ahmad ibn, *Musnad*, *I-VIII*, Beirut: al-Maktabat al-Islamiyya, 1993.

Bayhaqi, Abu Bakr Ahmad ibn Hussein ibn Ali, *al-Sunan al-Qubra, I-IX*, Dar al-Marifa, undated.

Bayhaqi, Abu Bakr Ahmad ibn Hussein ibn Ali, *Shu'ab al-Iman*, Beirut: Dar al-Kutub al-Ilmiyya, 1990.

Bukhari, Abu Abdullah Muhammad ibn Ismail, *Sahih al-Bukhari, I-VIII*, al-Maktabat al-Islamiyya, 1979.

Canan, Ibrahim, *Hadis Ansiklopedisi Kütüb-i Sitte, I-XVIII*, Akçağ, Ankara: 1989.

Jurjani, Al-Sayyid Sharif Ali ibn Muhammad, *al-Ta'rifat*, Beirut: 1983.

Hamdi Yazır, Hak Dini Kur'an Dili, 1-10, Istanbul: Eser Neşriyat, 1979.

Gülen, M. Fethullah, *Sonsuz Nur*, Izmir: Nil Yayınları, 2005.

Hakim, Abu Abdullah al-Naysaburi, *al-Mustadraq, I-V*; Beirut, Dar al-Marifa, 1986.

Haythami, Nuraddin Ali ibn Abu Bakr, *Majma al-Zawaid wa Manba al-Fawaid, I-X*, Beirut: Dar al-Kitab al-Arabi, 1967.

Hindi, Alaaddin Ali al-Muttaqi, *Kanz al-Ummal fi Sunan al-Aqwali wa al-Af'al, I-XVI*, Beirut: Muassasat al-Risala, 1985.

Ibn Abu Shayba Abdullah ibn Muhammad, *al-Musannaf, I-XIII*, Beirut: Dar al-Fikr, 1987.

Ibn al-Athir, Ali ibn Muhammad, *al-Kamil fi't Tarikh, I-XII*, Beirut: Dar al-Fikr, 1982.

Ibn Hajar, Shihab al-Din Abu al-Fadl Ahmad ibn Ali al-Askalani, *Fath al-Bari bi Sharhi Sahih al-Bukhari*, Egypt, 1959.

Ibn Hajar, Shihab al-Din Abu al-Fadl Ahmad ibn Ali al-Askalani, *al-Isaba fi Tamyiz al-Sahaba, I-IV*, Cairo: H. 1328.

Ibn Hibban, Abu Hatim ibn Hibban ibn Ahmad al-Tamimi, *al-Sahih*, Beirut: 1987.

Ibn Hisham, *al-Sirat al-Nabawiyya, I-IV*, Beirut: Dar al-Qalam, undated.

Ibn Kathir, Ismail ibn Umar, *al-Bidaya wa al-Nihaya, I-XIV*, Dar al-Kutub al-Ilmiyya, Beirut: 1988.

Ibn Maja, Abu Abdullah Muhammad ibn Yazid al-Kazwini, *al-Sunan*, al-Maktabat al-Islamiyya, Beirut: 1993.

Ibn Manzur, Abu al-Fadl Jamaladdin Muhammad ibn Mukarram, *Lisan al-Arab*, Dar al-Fikr, Beirut: 1990.

Konavi, Kasim, *Anis al-Fuqaha*, Dar al-Wafa, Jeddah: 1987.

Kutsal Kitap (Bible), Istanbul: Kitab-ı Mukaddes Şirketi, 1995.

Malik ibn Anas, Abu Abdullah, *al-Muwatta, I-II*, Dar al-Ihya al-Turas al-Arabi, Beirut: 1985.

Marghinani, Ali ibn Abu Bakr ibn Abd al-Jalil, *al-Hidaya Sharh al-Bidayat al-Mubtadi, I-IV*, Cairo: 1965.

Miras, Kamil, *Tecrid-i Sarih Tercemesi ve Şerhi*, Emel Matbaası, Ankara: 1975.

Munawi, Muhammad ibn Abdurrauf, *Fayz al-Qadir, I-VI*, Dar al-Kutub al-Ilmiyya, Beirut: 1994.

Muslim, Abu al-Hussain al-Hajjaj al-Naysaburi, *Sahih al-Muslim, I-V*, al-Maktabat al-Islamiyya, undated.

Nasai, Abu Abdurrahman ibn Shihab, *Sunan al-Nasai*, Egypt, 1964.

Sarahsi, Abu Bakr Muhammad ibn Abu Sahl, *Kitab al-Mabsut, I-XXX*, Dar al-Marifa, Beirut, undated.

Tahanawi, Muhammad Ali ibn Ali, *Kessafu Istilahati'l Funun, I-II*, Istanbul: 1984.

Tirmidhi, Muhammad ibn Isa, *al-Jami al-Sahih (Sunan)*, Dar al-Ihya al-Turas al-Arabi, Beirut, undated.

Yıldırım, Suat, *Kur'an-ı Hakim ve Açıklamalı Meali*, Işık Yayınları, Istanbul: 2003.

INDEX